CHILDCRAFT

THE HOW AND WHY LIBRARY

THE UNIVERSE

World Book, Inc.
a Scott Fetzer company
Chicago

Childcraft—The How and Why Library ISBN 0-7166-0197-4
The Universe ISBN 0-7166-0156-7
Library of Congress Catalog Card Number 98-75114
Printed in the United States of America
    2 3 4 5 6 7 8 9 06 05 04 03 02 01

**For information on other World Book products,
visit our Web site at www.worldbook.com
For information on sales to schools and libraries in the
United States, call 1-800-975-3250.
For information on sales to schools and libraries in
Canada, call 1-800-837-5365.**

Contents

Introduction 4

The Sun 8
Our sun is only one of countless stars in the universe. Find out what makes the sun more important than any other star.

The Moon 38
The moon is the brightest object in our night sky. Do you know why sometimes it is a huge, shining circle and other times a slim sliver? Do you know where it gets its light?

Our Solar System 62
Our solar system contains the sun and the many objects that travel around it. Learn about these objects, including our own planet, Earth!

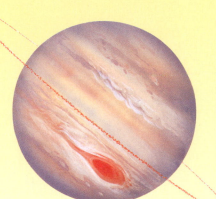

The Stars 98
Stars are balls of glowing gas in the sky. How many are there? How far away are they? What is a shooting star?

Studying the Universe . . 138
Since ancient times, people have studied heavenly bodies. You can study the heavenly bodies, too!

Glossary 184

Index 188

Illustration Acknowledgments . . 192

Introduction

Twinkle, twinkle, little star, how I wonder what you are. Have you ever sung that song? You probably have, because ever since you were little, you have seen light coming from shiny objects high in the sky. The sun shines in the daytime, the stars shine at night, and the moon sometimes glows day and night. As you got older, you learned that those objects are far, far away. You learned that you live on the planet Earth. And you learned that Earth and all the other planets and stars are part of one huge universe.

This book, *The Universe*, explores the sun, the moon, the planets, and the stars. In the pages that follow, you will find out what these heavenly bodies are made of and how scientists study them. You will also read stories that people around the world have told over the years to explain such things as the movement of the sun and the changing shape of the moon.

People have been watching the sky for thousands of years. In this book, you will meet some of history's most famous astronomers—scientists who studied the universe and made important discoveries. You will learn how a telescope works and find out what it is like to travel in space. Maybe someday you might even want to work in space. There is still so much to explore in the universe!

Certain features of this book can help you find your way through it. You will find fun-filled facts in the boxes marked **Know It All!** You can amaze your friends with what you learn!

This book also has many activities that you can do at home. Look for the words **Try This!** over a colored ball. The activity that follows offers a way to learn about the universe. For example, you can make a

hanging model of the planets in the solar system. You can set up a simple telescope. Or you can grow food without soil, as if you were living in space.

Each activity has a number in its colored ball. Activities with a 1 in a green ball are simplest to do. Those with a 2 in a yellow ball may require a little adult help with tasks such as cutting, measuring, or using hot water. Activities with a 3 in a red ball may need more adult help.

A Try This! activity that has a colorful border around its entire page is a little more complex or requires a few more materials. Take a moment to review the list of materials needed and to read through the step-by-step instructions before you begin.

As you read this book, you will see that some words are printed in bold type, **like this**. These are words that might be new to you. You can find the meanings and pronunciations of these words in the **Glossary** at the back of the book. Turn to the **Index** to look up page numbers of subjects that particularly interest you.

If you enjoy learning about the universe, find out more about it in other resources. Here are just a few. Check

them out at a bookstore or at your local or school library.

📖 **Asteroids, Comets, and Meteors,** by Gregory L. Vogt, 1996. *You will learn many interesting facts about asteroids, comets, and meteors, including what they are, what they look like, and where they come from.*

📖 **If You Were an Astronaut,** by Virginia Schomp, 1998. *The training to be an astronaut, the launch, and the mission are explained in this colorful book.*

📼 **The Magic School Bus Gets Lost in Space,** by Brian Meehl and Jocelyn Stevenson, 1995. *Video 30 minutes.*

📖 **Mars,** by Larry Dane Brimmer, 1998. *In simple-to-understand language for the young astronomer, this book tells of the planet Mars as well as past and future explorations. See the other books on planets in the "A True Book" series.*

📖 **The Moon,** by Carmen Bredeson, 1998. *The older child will enjoy this book about the history of the moon, its physical makeup, the Apollo Space program, and what we have learned from these missions.*

📖 **Night Sky,** by Carole Stott, 1993. *You can be a sky watcher, and this book will tell you what to look for.*

🔷 **The Nine Planets,** http://www.seds.org/nineplanets/ nineplanets/   *This Web site takes you on a multimedia tour of the solar system and all its planets and moons.*

📖 **The Seasons of Arnold's Apple Tree,** by Gail Gibbons, 1984. *This picture book by a popular author tells of a young boy enjoying his apple tree during the different seasons.*

🕸 **SpaceQuest Planetarium,** http://www.nasa.gov/ *The ultimate Web site for information on space exploration.*

📖 **Stargazers,** by Gail Gibbons, 1992. *Even the youngest child can enjoy this book that tells about constellations and explains how telescopes work.*

📖 **The Universe,** by Gallemaid Jeunesse and Jean-Pierre Verdet, 1995. *This very basic book on the universe for the young child has brightly colored transparent pages to make the discovery of the universe even more exciting.*

8

The Sun

Up in the sky, there is a big yellow ball, the sun. It is only one of millions of stars in the universe. But the sun is more important to people than any other star. Without the sun's heat and light, there could be no life on Earth.

What Is the Sun?

The sun is a star. It is the closest star to Earth. Our word *sun* comes from the word *Sol* (sahl). Sol was the name of the ancient Roman sun god. From the name Sol comes our word *solar* (SOH luhr), which means "of the sun." And our **solar system** includes everything that moves around the sun.

The sun glows because it is extremely hot. The sun's center, its core, is a kind of giant furnace in which the temperature is about 27 million °F (15 million °C).

The sun may not look it, but it is huge. At least 333,000 **planets** the size of Earth could fit into the sun. Why doesn't the sun look huge to us? The farther away something is, the smaller it appears. And the sun is about 93 million miles (150 million kilometers) from Earth!

Water freezes at 32 °F (0 °C). Water boils at 212 °F (100 °C). The sun's temperature at its center is about 27 million °F (15 million °C).

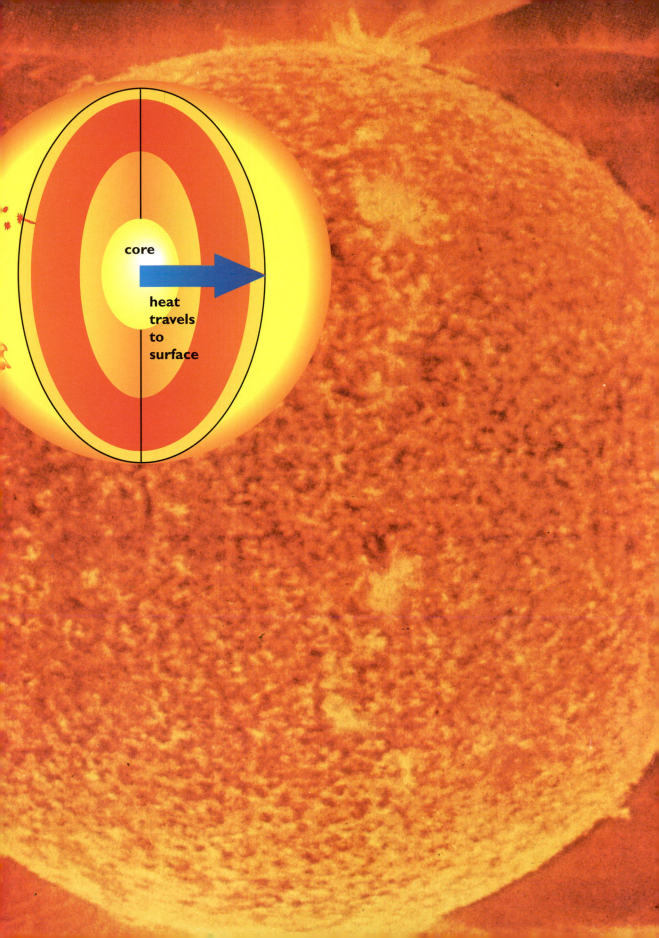

core

heat
travels
to
surface

How Was the Sun Formed?

Most scientists think our sun began as a gigantic cloud of **gas** and dust.

Stars that are growing old often shoot out huge clouds of gases and dust. The gases and dust are made up of all kinds of chemicals. As these gas-and-dust clouds move through space, they pull more and more gases and dust into themselves.

Within each cloud, all the gases and dust come closer and closer together. Over many millions of years, the center of the cloud is pulled into the shape of a huge ball. The ball's center becomes more dense, or packed, than a ball of steel. When gas is squeezed together that much, it becomes very hot. The tiniest parts of some of the gases begin to join together. The ball becomes even hotter and begins to glow.

This is how all new stars seem to form. Most scientists think this is how our own sun began, over 4 1/2 billion years ago.

Energy
from
the sun
goes to . . .

Why Is the Sun Important?

Without the sun, most plants and animals would not survive.

Energy comes up from inside the raging hot center of the sun. It reaches the sun's boiling, bubbling surface. Then it shoots out into space as light.

The sun's light spreads out in all directions. It travels at 186,282 miles (299,792 kilometers) per second. That is about 10 million times faster than most cars move along a freeway.

How do plants make energy from sunlight? Plants are like factories where food is made. Green leaves are made up of millions of tiny cells, like little bags. When sunlight passes into a leaf, those tiny cells catch and hold the sun's energy. Using the captured sunlight for power, the plant's cells turn water and a gas from the air into a kind of sugar. The sugar is stored-up energy that is used by the plant.

Much of the sun's light speeds on into the endless darkness of space. But some heads straight for Earth. It passes through our sky and travels down to us. Here it strikes leaves and blades of grass. Plants use the sun's energy to make their own food and to grow.

. . . plants on Earth.

Once a plant has grown, perhaps cattle will eat it. Now the cattle will have the plant's energy. In time, the bodies of the cattle may be turned into steaks and hamburgers for people to eat. The energy that came from the sun will then go into people's bodies. People will use this energy to work or play.

Energy from plants goes into cattle.

Energy from meat goes into people!

Of course, people also eat plants. When that happens, the people get energy straight from the plants.

All living things must take in energy to stay alive. And nearly all energy comes from the sun. So the sun gives us much more than just light and heat. It truly gives us life.

Why Does the Sun Disappear at Night?

The sun does not really disappear at night. It just seems to vanish, because the part of Earth you live on has turned away from it.

Earth is slowly turning all the time. When it is morning, the part of Earth you live on is starting to face the sun. The sun seems low in the sky. As the day goes on, Earth goes on turning, and the sun appears higher in the sky. When your part of the world is directly in line with the sun, it is the time of day we call noon.

When it is night in your part of the world, you get ready for bed. But halfway around the world, other children are waking up.

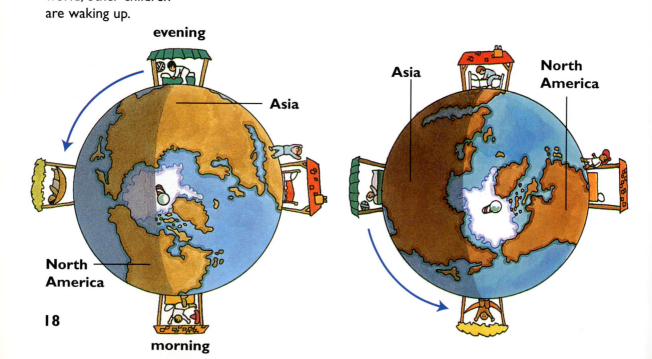

evening

Asia

North America

morning

Asia

North America

18

Earth continues to turn. Slowly your part of Earth moves away from the sun. That is why it gets darker and the sun seems to go down. Soon your part of Earth is completely away from the sun, and it is night.

Half of Earth is always getting light from the sun. The other half is always dark. As your part of Earth moves away from the sun, the other side is beginning to face the sun. There, the day is just beginning.

TRY THIS!

2

When it is the middle of the day for you, it is the middle of the night on the other side of the world! Can you find the city that is on the opposite side of the globe from you? On a globe, find your city or the point closest to your town. Next, take two pieces of string. Wrap one piece from your town around the top and bottom of the globe. Wrap the other piece from your town around the "side." The two pieces meet at two points. One point is your home. The other point is the other side of the world from you.

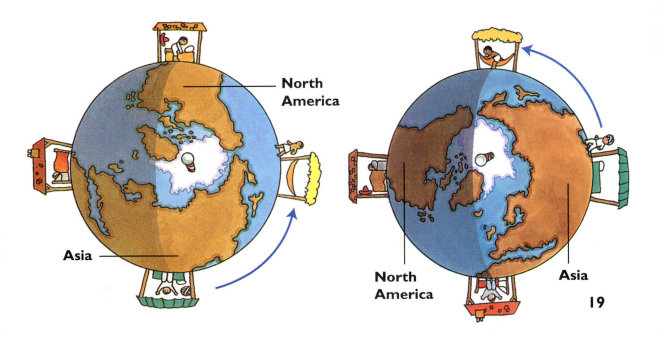

North America

Asia

North America

Asia

What is your shadow? You make a shadow when your body gets in the way of shining light. Your shadow is the dark patch that shows up when the light can't get through you.

morning shadow

Where's Your Shadow?

Take a walk outdoors early on a sunny morning, and your shadow will follow long and to one side. Later in the day, while you're playing, your shadow becomes short and almost seems to hide. You can probably stretch your leg over your shadow's head. Later, just before sunset, your shadow friend will be long and to the other side of you. Why does your shadow grow and shrink while you stay exactly the same size?

Your shadow's size has to do with the sun's position in the sky. Every day the sun appears to move across the sky. It rises in the east and sets in the west.

noon shadow

evening shadow

When the sun first comes up in the morning, it is very low in the sky. Most of your body blocks some light, so your shadow is very tall. And since the sun always rises in the east, your morning shadow will always be to the west.

As the morning turns to noon, the sun gets higher in the sky, and your shadow becomes shorter. By noon, the sun almost forms a straight line with your body. Your body is blocking very little light from the sun. This makes your shadow very short.

As afternoon passes, the sun's position continues to move across the sky. The sun moves downward, and your shadow grows taller again, this time to the east. By the time the sun is ready to set in the evening, it is very low in the sky, and your shadow will once again be very tall. As it gets dark, your shadow disappears.

TRY THIS!

1

Find a sunny sidewalk with a friend. Be sure there are no trees or buildings that will block the sun at all during the day. Have your friend trace around your shadow in the morning, at noon, and late in the afternoon. Trace your friend's shadow, too. When are the shadows biggest? When are they smallest?

What Are Seasons?

Summer—trees burst with thick loads of leaves. Flowers nod in soft, warm breezes. Insects buzz. A blue sky holds a bright, hot sun.

Winter—bare trees stand like bony skeletons against the cold, gray sky. Snow blankets the ground. The sun seems pale and far away.

spring

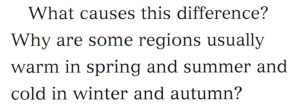

summer

What causes this difference? Why are some regions usually warm in spring and summer and cold in winter and autumn?

Summer comes to your part of the world when daylight begins early and stretches to almost bedtime or even later. The sunlight is also stronger. Winter comes when not as much of the sun's light reaches your part of the world.

fall

Daylight hours are few in winter. It may be dark when you wake up, and dark when you get home from school. The ground and air cool off.

The difference in the amount of sunlight each season has is caused by the tilt of the planet Earth. While Earth is spinning in space, it is also traveling around the sun. The way the planet tilts as it travels around the sun causes the seasons.

As Earth moves, it spins like a top. It turns around an imaginary line called an **axis** (AK sihs). We think of this axis like a pole. We call the top the **North Pole** and we call the other end the **South Pole.**

Earth's axis is tilted, the way a top tilts when it is about to stop. When the North Pole is tilted toward the sun, the northern half of Earth gets more sunlight, and the

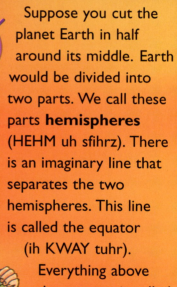

summer in the north

winter in the south

Suppose you cut the planet Earth in half around its middle. Earth would be divided into two parts. We call these parts **hemispheres** (HEHM uh sfihrz). There is an imaginary line that separates the two hemispheres. This line is called the equator (ih KWAY tuhr). Everything above the equator is called the Northern Hemisphere, and everything below is called the Southern Hemisphere.

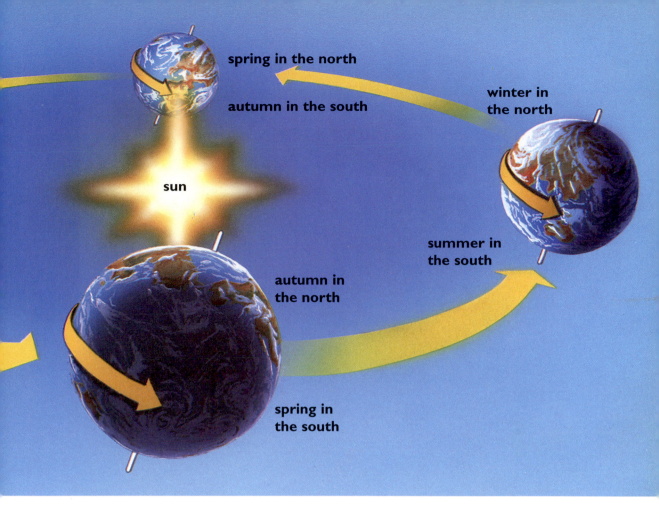

spring in the north

autumn in the south

winter in
the north

sun

summer in
the south

autumn in
the north

spring in
the south

southern half gets less sunlight. This makes it summer in the north and winter in the south.

Slowly, Earth moves around the sun. Soon the North Pole begins to tilt away from the sun. As this happens, the southern half tilts toward the sun. Then the northern half gets colder. It becomes autumn, then winter, in the north. And the southern half gets warmer. It becomes spring, then summer, in the south.

Where Is the Sun?

In an eclipse, *above,* light from the sun creates a ring effect as the moon passes between the sun and the planet Earth.

It is the middle of the day. The sun hangs bright in the sky. Suddenly, the sky seems to be growing dark! The sun seems to be disappearing! Soon the sun is nearly as dark as night and there is only a pale, fuzzy ring around it! What has happened?

The **moon**, which moves around the planet Earth, has passed between Earth and the sun. The sun is much bigger than the moon, but it is so far away from us that the moon seems to cover it up. When the moon is between the sun and Earth, the moon throws a shadow on Earth. The part of Earth covered by the shadow gets dark. This is a total **eclipse** (ih KLIHPS) of the sun, or a total solar eclipse.

Sometimes the moon covers only part of the sun. This is called a partial (PAHR shuhl) eclipse.

The sun's rays can hurt your eyes, so never look directly at the sun—even during an eclipse!

sun

moon's shadow

Earth

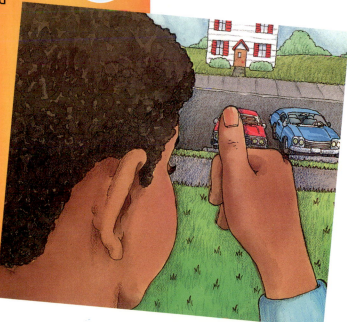

TRY THIS!

1

The next time you are outdoors, look at a house in your neighborhood. Hold your hand in front of one eye so that you block your view of the house. Your hand is smaller than the house, but it is still blocking some of the house from your view. That is because the house is pretty far away. The farther away the house is, the more of it your hand can block. The moon, which is much smaller than the sun, can eclipse the sun in the same way.

Myths About the Sun

Long ago, people in many cultures throughout the world worshiped the sun. No wonder! Like us, they could not live without it. They depended on it for light, warmth, and even food. The following tales tell about the sun gods of some long-ago peoples.

Old Man Sun lived among the San, wanderers in Africa's Kalahari Desert. Light shone from his armpits whenever he raised his arms. The San children lifted the old man while he slept and threw him into the sky, where his light could shine on everyone.

The sun god of the Zuni, a Native American people, sent his sons to Earth's

people, who lived underground. The sons
led the people on a difficult journey to the
surface of the planet Earth. When they
arrived, even the light of the morning stars
hurt their eyes. And when the sun first
rose, they cried out in pain. But soon they
could look around and see the many
beautiful things in their new world.

How did early people explain the sun moving across the sky? The Greeks thought the sun god Helios drove it every day in a chariot across the heavens. The Egyptians said the sun god Re (ray) brought light to the world by sailing the sun across the sky in his boat each day. The Maoris of New Zealand believed one of their heroes had fought the sun and crippled it, so that it limped across the sky.

Some peoples believed that an eclipse was a sign that the sun god was angry with them. They believed that prayer and offerings would calm the sun god.

The ancient Chinese had a different belief. They thought a dragon was actually eating the sun during an eclipse. They made noise to scare off the dragon so that it would leave the sun alone.

A Japanese story says that the first eclipse happened when Amaterasu, the sun goddess, hid in a cave. The other gods began singing, dancing, and laughing just outside the cave. Curious about the uproar, Amaterasu peered out and was surprised to see her own reflection in a mirror that the gods had made. As she paused, one of the gods took her hand and pulled her outside. The eclipse was over.

Maui Tames the Sun

This folk tale about the movement of the sun is from the Pacific Islands.

Long ago, when the planet Earth was young, the sun sailed across the sky very fast. No matter how early people got out of bed, they couldn't get enough work done because the sun would disappear. One evening, Maui told his brothers that he could tame the sun.

Maui asked his brothers to make a rope out of coconut fibers. But the fibers

would not hold the sun. Then he had his
brothers make a rope out of vines. But
the rope would not hold the sun. Finally,
Maui's mother cut her hair and wove it
into a net. This time, when the sun
zoomed along, the net of hair caught it.
Maui told the sun he would let it go if it
promised to slow down. The sun agreed,
and that is why we have time to work,
play, and rest during the day.

The Sun Has Chickenpox!

Have you ever had chickenpox? If you have, you probably remember that parts of your body were covered with spots. Scientists who study the sun say that sometimes it looks as if the sun has chickenpox, too!

But the sun's dark spots, called **sunspots**, are not caused by a virus the way chickenpox is. Sunspots are caused by giant storms on the sun's surface.

From Earth, these storms look like dark dots because they are much cooler than the rest of the sun's blazing hot surface.

Most sunspots start off in pairs and drift apart. Because they are so far away from us, they look small. But just one of these spots is bigger than the whole Earth!

Sunspots do not occur all the time. Sometimes, the sun's surface is covered with them. Years later, there may be very few. Scientists have learned that they run in **cycles** of about 11 years.

This picture was taken through a special camera that is able to show the cooler spots on the sun's surface. The yellow and red areas are sunspots.

The dark spots that sometimes appear on the sun's surface are caused by huge storms.

Too Much Sun Can Hurt Us

The sun is important for all living things. But too much of it can be dangerous.

The sun sends out invisible rays of light called ultraviolet rays. These ultraviolet rays often tan the skin of people who sit in the sun. But if we stay in the sun too long without protecting our skin, these rays can burn our skin. They can even cause skin cancer.

How can you protect your skin from sun damage? First, when you are in the sun, remember to cover your skin as much as possible and wear sunscreen. This will help block the harmful rays.

Sometimes ultraviolet rays can hurt your eyes or make them puffy. You can help protect your eyes from the sun by wearing sunglasses. And never look straight at the sun. Do not even look at an area of the sky close to the sun! It will damage your eyes. Scientists study sunspots safely by using solar telescopes and other special equipment.

The Moon

The moon is the brightest object in our night sky. On some nights, the moon looks like a huge shining circle of light. On other nights, it looks like a thin, silver fingernail. But the moon does not really change its size or shape. And it does not make its own light. The light we see comes from the sun and bounces off the moon.

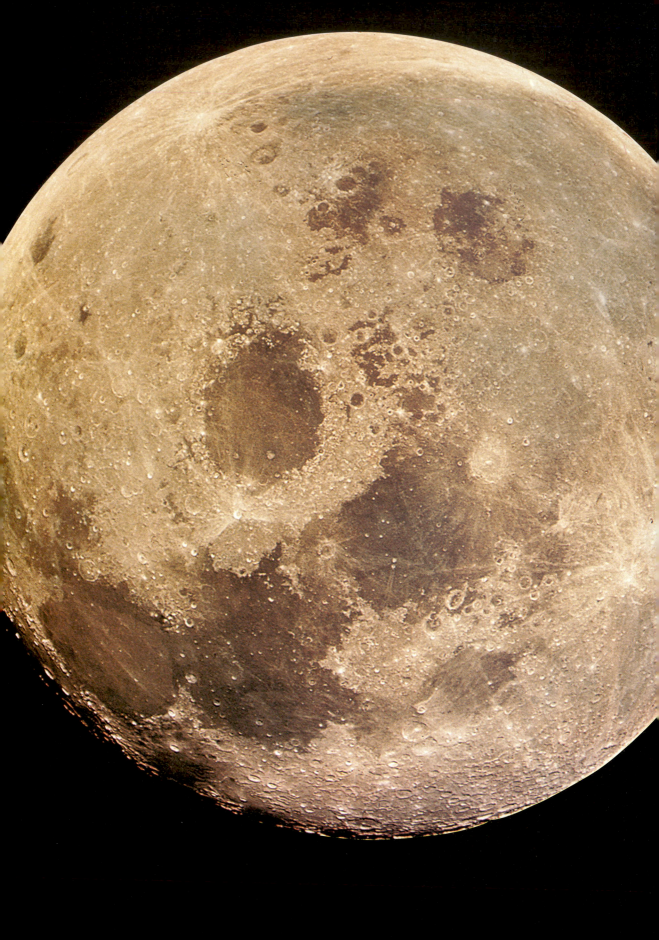

What Is the Moon?

The stars are trillions of miles away. The sun is millions of miles away. But the **moon** is only about 239,000 miles (384,000 kilometers) away. As Earth moves through space, the moon is always beside it. The moon moves around Earth.

The moon is smaller than most **planets** and stars. If Earth were the size of a basketball, the moon would be about the size of a tennis ball.

The moon is a ball of gray rock. Some of it is covered with dust. It has no air and no water. Most living things that we know of could not survive on the moon.

Long ago, many groups of people worshiped the moon. The ancient Romans named the moon Luna. Our word *lunar* (LOO nuhr) means "of the moon."

The full moon was photographed by the spacecraft Apollo 11 as it sped homeward after the first landing on the moon.

Moon

Earth

KNOW It All!

What holds the moon in place? The moon is held in place by the tug of Earth's stronger **gravity** (GRAV uh tee). Gravity is the natural force that draws things toward Earth's surface or toward each other. An object that is held by a planet this way is called a **satellite** (SAT uh lyt). The moon is Earth's satellite.

Myths About the Moon

Imagine that you lived in the world more than 2,000 years ago. Every night the moon appeared, but you had no idea what it was or why it seemed to change shape. Would you make up a story to explain it? Many ancient people did.

Some early people thought the moon was a powerful god or goddess. The ancient Romans called their moon goddesses Luna and Diana. Diana was also the goddess of the hunt. The crescent moon was her bow, and the moonbeams were her arrows.

Some ancient people had stories about the moon and the sun together. Some Native Americans believed that the moon and the sun were brother and sister gods.

TRY THIS!

1

On a clear night, especially a night when the moon is full or almost full, look carefully to see what shapes you can find on the moon's surface. If you have a telescope or binoculars, use them. Use your imagination. What do you see? Can you see the "man in the moon"?

Some sky gazers saw figures like a cat, a frog, or a rabbit in the moon's markings. Others saw the face of a man. Legends of various lands told how the "man in the moon" had been put in prison for stealing or for breaking religious rules.

Was there once life on the moon? Some cultures believed there was. A Greek writer named Plutarch told of moon demons that lived in caves. A German astronomer in the 1800's, F. P. Gruithuisen, told of seeing a city on the moon through a telescope.

Even today, some cultures use stories to explain why the moon seems to change shape.

Can you see the rabbit that some sky gazers saw in the moon?

The San people of southern Africa tell one story that explains why the moon seems to change its shape. This story says that each month the moon almost dies. But it is reborn just in time to start life all over again. When this happens, it is seen as a thin sliver. For 13 nights, it grows until it becomes a full moon. The San celebrate this with three nights of dancing.

Then the moon begins to die again. For the next 13 nights, the sun, which the San see as the great hunter, battles the moon. Slowly the great hunter slices at the moon, until there is no moon left. For a few days, the moon seems to be dead. But soon it is reborn, and it begins growing again.

Why Does the Moon Shine?

The moon is reflecting light from the sun. The water is reflecting light from the moon.

The moon is made of cold, hard rock. It is not a ball of hot, glowing **gas** like the sun. Yet, somehow, the moon shines.

But the moon doesn't give off its own light. It reflects (ree FLEHKTS) light from the sun. That means light from the sun bounces off the surface of the moon and some of that light reaches Earth.

The moon does not really reflect sunlight very well. Most of the rock on the moon is rough and dark gray, not smooth and shiny like a mirror. But the sun's light is so bright that even the tiny bit that is reflected from the moon makes the moon appear to be glowing.

Earth shines, too! It reflects some of the sunlight that falls on it.

This part of Earth is sunny.

The moon reflects light from the sun.

This part of Earth is dark. It receives no sunlight, only light from the moon.

Here there is no sunlight and no moonlight.

An Eclipse of the Moon

The night is clear, and a bright, full moon is shining. Slowly, a dark shadow begins to fall across the face of the moon. The shadow seems to move along until it completely covers the moon.

This event is called an eclipse of the moon, a **lunar eclipse**. It takes place when Earth comes between the moon and the sun. The shadow creeping across the moon is the shadow of Earth!

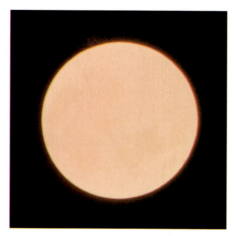

When Earth passes between the sun and the full moon, Earth's shadow falls across the surface of the moon.

As the eclipse begins, the shadow of Earth falls on the moon.

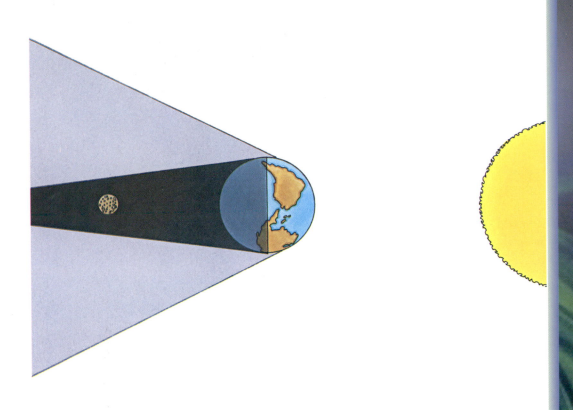

The shadow of Earth grows...

until it almost covers, or eclipses, the moon.

Phases of the Moon

The moon seems to change from a thin crescent to a full circle. Each time the moon looks different, we say it is in a new phase. A phase is a change in the moon's shape as it is seen from Earth.

1. In the moon's first phase, it can't be seen at all. That is because the moon is between Earth and the sun. The sun is shining on the side of the moon that faces the sun, but there is no sunlight on the side that faces us. So all we see is darkness.

2. After a day or two, the moon moves to one side of us. Then we can see a tiny bit of the side that is lit by the sun. We call this phase a crescent moon.

Oh! Look at the Moon

by *Eliza Lee Follen*

Oh! look at the moon,
She is shining up there;
Oh! Mother, she looks
Like a lamp in the air.

Last week she was smaller
And shaped like a bow;
But now she's grown bigger,
And round as an O.

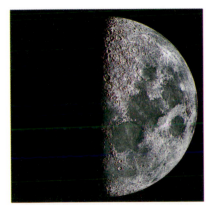

3. After about seven days, we can see half of the moon's sunlit side. This phase is called a half moon.

4. After about two weeks, the moon is halfway around Earth from where it started. Now we can see the whole side of the moon that the sun is shining on. We call this phase a full moon. The moon keeps moving, and the part we can see gets smaller and smaller. Finally, the moon is between Earth and the sun again.

51

TRY THIS!

1

Do-It-Yourself Phases of the Moon

Why does the moon have phases? See for yourself by doing this experiment.

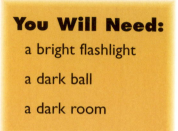

You Will Need:

a bright flashlight

a dark ball

a dark room

What To Do:

1. Place the flashlight on a table or shelf. Set the ball on a surface of the same height. Then shine the light on it. The flashlight acts as the sun. The ball is the moon. You are the planet Earth.

2. Sit directly between the light and the front of the ball, but beneath the beam of light. The whole side of the ball facing you will be in light, like a full moon is.

full moon

half moon

3. Move to the "side" of the ball. You will see half of the ball in the light, like a half moon.

crescent moon

4. Move around the ball a little more, so that the ball is nearly between you and the light. Most of the ball will be in shadow. Only a small part will be in the light, like a crescent moon.

Now you know why the moon has different phases. The moon and Earth change positions. Use this activity to explain it to a friend.

Was there ever life on the moon? We know that living things need water to survive. Since no scientists have proven that there was ever water on the moon, we can guess there have been no living things on the moon either.

The surface of the moon is full of craters, or holes. It also has plains, mountains, and boulders. The huge boulder shown here towers over the astronaut and his land rover vehicle.

What Is the Moon Like?

The surface of the moon is not the same all over. In some areas, it has broad, flat plains covered with powdery rock dust. In other areas, it has rugged mountains. It also has billions of round holes in the ground called craters (KRAY tuhrs).

Some of the craters are no bigger than a pencil point. Some are the size of a car tire. And some are bigger than the Grand Canyon! The biggest crater on the moon is over 700 miles (1,100 kilometers) across.

What formed the moon's craters and mountains? Chunks of rock called **meteoroids** (MEE tee uh royds) move around the sun, just as Earth and the moon do. Sometimes these meteoroids crash into the moon. The moon and the meteoroids are moving so fast that the meteoroids make craters in the moon's surface when they crash.

When meteoroids strike, they usually form walls of rock around the craters they make. Many of the moon's mountains are really walls made by meteors.

There is no wind to disturb the dust on the moon, so this astronaut's footprint is probably still there.

What Would It Be Like to Live on the Moon?

Life on the moon would be dark, quiet, and uncomfortable. But living there would definitely improve your high jump!

Earth's sky looks blue during the day because the air on Earth scatters blue

Mining on the moon? Maybe someday. This is one artist's drawing of what mining on the moon might look like. The moon is rich in resources.

light from the sun in all directions. But there is no air on the moon to scatter sunlight, so its sky is pitch-black. On Earth, air carries sound. On the moon, no sound can be heard.

During the day, the moon's surface gets hotter than boiling water. During the night, the moon is colder than the coldest place on Earth.

We are held on the surface of Earth by the pull of Earth's gravity. When we weigh ourselves, we are really measuring how hard the gravity is tugging on us.

The moon's gravity is weaker than Earth's gravity. On the moon, you would weigh one-sixth as much as you weigh on Earth. If you weigh 60 pounds (27 kilograms) on Earth, you would weigh only 10 pounds (4.5 kilograms) on the moon! You could also jump six times higher on the moon than you could on Earth. And you could lift objects that you couldn't even budge at home on Earth.

The moon turns slowly. The daylight part of one moon day is about as long as 14 earth-days. So if you lived on the moon, it would be daytime for 14 days in a row! And nighttime on the moon is just as long.

An astronaut collects samples from the moon during the Apollo 15 mission in 1971.

High Tide, Low Tide

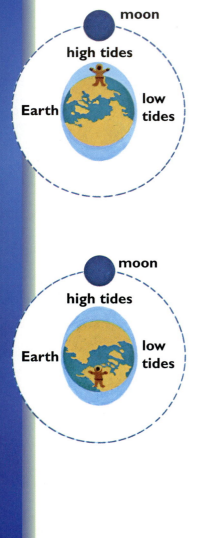

The regular rise and fall of the ocean is called the tide. The tide is caused mostly by forces of gravity from the moon. These forces produce two high tides and two low tides each day.

High tide takes place on the part of Earth that is nearest to the moon. At the same time, high tide also takes place on the part of Earth farthest from the moon.

This seems strange, but there are several reasons for tides. An important one is the way the moon's gravity pulls on Earth.

On the side of Earth closer to the moon, the moon's pull is slightly stronger than it is in the center of Earth. On the opposite side of Earth, the moon's pull is slightly weaker. High tide happens where the moon's pull is strongest and also where it is weakest.

As Earth turns, the water sinks back down. After about six hours, this part of the sea is all the way down to what is called low tide.

high tide

low tide

Moons of Other Planets

Earth is not the only planet that has a moon. Six other planets do, too!

Mars has two little moons that are just lumpy chunks of rock. The largest, Phobos, is only about 14 miles (22 kilometers) wide. Mars's other moon, Deimos, is about 9 miles (14 kilometers) wide.

Phobos

Jupiter, *upper right*, has four planet-sized moons.

Just how big are Mars's moons? On a map, find the island of Manhattan in New York City, New York. Manhattan is about 13 1/2 miles (21.7 kilometers) long. So Mars's larger moon, Phobos, is about as wide as Manhattan is long! Deimos is a little more than half that size.

Jupiter has 16 moons. The smallest, Sinope, is smaller than

some of the mountains on Earth.
But the biggest, Ganymede, is
bigger than the planets Mercury
and Pluto.

Saturn has 18 moons. Like
Jupiter's moons, Saturn's are very
different in size. Five are smaller
than 25 miles (40 kilometers) wide.
The biggest moon, Titan, is bigger
than Earth's moon. Titan is also bigger
than Mercury or Pluto.

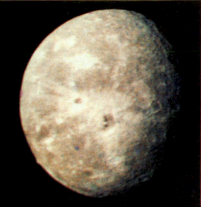

Oberon is one of the
moons of the planet
Uranus.

Saturn, *center*, and some of its many moons

Our Solar System

Our solar system contains the sun and the many objects that travel around it. Some are planets much larger than Earth. Others are tiny meteors and bits of dust.

The Sun's Family

There are nine **planets** in our solar system. Each of them moves around the sun in a certain path. This path is called an **orbit** (AWR biht).

The first two planets, Mercury and Venus, are very close to the sun. The others are much farther away. Three planets are much smaller than Earth. One is about the same size. And four are much bigger.

Like Earth and the moon, the other planets in our solar system reflect the sun's light. That's why we can see some of them at night.

The sun's family also includes **asteroids**, **comets**, and **meteoroids**. Asteroids (AS tuh roydz) are small masses of rock or metal. Most

Comet

Jupiter

Sun

Mercury

Venus

Earth

Mars

Asteroid belt

of them move around the sun between the orbits of Mars and Jupiter.

Comets (KAHM ihts) are frozen balls of ice, gas, and dust that travel

Pluto

Neptune

Uranus

Saturn

around the sun. Comets have long shining tails.

Meteoroids (MEE tee uh roydz) are chunks of rock or metal that move through space. When a meteoroid enters Earth's **atmosphere** from outer space and begins to burn, it becomes a bright streak called a shooting star, or meteor (MEE tee uhr).

TRY THIS!
1

Use words that begin with the letters m, v, e, m, j, s, u, n, and p—in that order—to form a fun sentence. Memorize the sentence. When you need to remember the planets in order, just think of your sentence and the first letter of each word. Here is an example: **M**iss **V**iolet **E**njoys **M**unching **J**elly **S**andwiches **U**nder **N**eighbors' **P**orches! Now you try.

Mercury, Closest to the Sun

Mercury

Earth

Do you know someone who often changes quickly like the temperature on Mercury? If so, you could say that person is mercurial!

Mercury is the nearest planet to the sun. It is a bare rocky ball covered with craters, much like our moon. Also like our moon, Mercury has broad, flat plains and steep cliffs.

Mercury spins and has day and night, but it spins very slowly. One day on Mercury takes 59 earth-days.

Mercury is very hot during the day. Temperatures there reach higher than 800 °F (400 °C). At night, temperatures take a big dip, sometimes to nearly -280 °F (-170 °C)!

Mercury has a bigger temperature change than any other planet. This is because it is closest to the sun, and because it has very long days.

Mercury is a small planet. It could fit inside Earth two and one-half times. There are hardly any gases surrounding Mercury, so it has very little atmosphere.

Length of day:
59 earth-days

Length of year:
88 earth-days

Number of moons:
0

Mercury is much closer to the sun than Earth is. So if you were standing on Mercury, the sun would appear much bigger and brighter.

Of course, you could not stand on Mercury in the middle of the day or night because it is either too hot or too cold. But scientists have explored it with a spacecraft that had no people aboard.

Even if it were possible to sunbathe on Mercury, it wouldn't be a good idea. Mercury is much too close to the sun for people to enjoy its rays.

The U.S. Mariner 10 became the first and only spacecraft to reach Mercury. Mariner 10 was a space probe (prohb). A space probe is a machine that explores space and sends information and pictures back to Earth. Astronauts do not travel in space probes. Scientists on Earth use computers to control space probes. On March 29, 1974, Mariner 10 flew within 460 miles (740 kilometers) of Mercury. It swept past the planet again on September 24, 1974, and on March 16, 1975. During these flights, the probe took photographs of parts of Mercury's surface. In the future, more space probes may go into orbit around Mercury, or land on it.

Venus – Earth's "Twin"

Venus is nearly the same size as Earth, so it is often called Earth's "twin." But it is nothing at all like our world. Venus's atmosphere is full of poisonous gases. Its clouds contain a chemical strong enough to dissolve metal! And the clouds on Venus are so thick that cameras can't see the planet's surface.

High in Venus's atmosphere, powerful windstorms are raging. Venus's windstorms are much worse than storms on Earth. Lightning flashes in the sky as often as 20 times a minute.

Venus is the second closest planet to the sun. This makes it extremely hot and dry. As seen from Earth, Venus is brighter than all the other planets and stars. It is so bright that it can sometimes be seen in the daytime! A year on Venus is as long as 225 earth-days. Like Mercury, Venus has no moons.

Venus

Earth

Length of day:
243 earth-days

Length of year:
225 earth-days

Number of moons:
0

KNOW It All!

Scientists once thought the planet Venus would be much like Earth, but warmer. They were wrong. Venus is extremely hot, and its atmosphere is very heavy. The first few space probes scientists sent to Venus were squashed by its atmosphere before they could send back information.

Length of day:
24 hours

Length of year:
365 days

Number of moons:
one

Earth

Earth is a watery planet. More than two-thirds of Earth's surface is covered with water. That's good for all the living things in our world because animals and plants need water to live. Animals and plants live almost everywhere on Earth.

Earth

Earth is the third planet from the sun, and air surrounds it. The air is made up of gases, such as **oxygen**, **nitrogen**, and **carbon dioxide**. These gases are needed for almost all living things to survive. Human beings breathe in oxygen. Plants need carbon dioxide.

If you look at a globe, you will find the **North Pole** on one end and the **South Pole** on the other. Earth looks like a ball, but it is actually a little flatter at the North and South poles.

Earth travels 595 million miles (958 million kilometers) around the sun. It takes about 365 days for Earth to orbit the sun once. That's why there are about 365 days in an earth-year.

Earth is at least 4 ½ billion years old!

Length of day:
24 hours, 37 minutes

Length of year:
About 1 earth-year and
10 ½ months

Number of moons:
two

Mars, the Red Planet

Mars

Earth

Mars is the fourth planet from the sun. It is also known as the red planet because it has a reddish tint. What makes Mars red? Its dry, desertlike regions are covered by rust-colored dust, sand, and rocks. Fierce windstorms whirl the orange-colored sand up from the plains and fill the air with dust. This dust gives the Martian sky a reddish color as well.

There are many canyons, craters, and volcanoes on Mars. One volcano, called Olympus Mons, is nearly three times as high as Mount Everest, the highest mountain on Earth. In fact, Olympus Mons is the largest volcano in the entire solar system!

Mars is only about half the size of Earth and has two small moons. The largest, called Phobos, is about 14 miles (22 kilometers) wide. The other, Deimos, is about 7 miles (11 kilometers) wide.

Mars has craters that are many times deeper than any craters on Earth.

75

Is There Life on Mars?

Mars is more like Earth than any other planet. It is farther from the sun than Mercury or Venus, so it is not as hot as they are. Its atmosphere is thinner than the air on Earth, but some kinds of living things could survive in it. That's why some scientists believe that life may once have existed on Mars.

The Pathfinder spacecraft took these pictures of the mountains and boulders on Mars. Near right is the the rolling Sojourner robot.

In 1976, two U.S. space probes named Viking 1 and Viking 2 landed on the red planet. Neither of these two probes found any evidence of life.

In 1984, however, a small meteorite—about as big as a potato—was found in Antarctica. A meteorite is a meteoroid that lands on Earth. Scientists believed that this meteorite came from the planet Mars. In 1996, some scientists said they could tell from this meteorite that there had once been life on Mars. The meteorite had material on it that seemed similar to substances that come from some tiny living things on Earth. Other scientists disagreed that these substances showed the existence of life on Mars.

On July 4, 1997, a U.S. space probe called the Mars Pathfinder visited the red planet. When the Pathfinder landed, its doors opened and a small six-wheeled vehicle rolled out and began exploring. The vehicle, called Sojourner, looked like a remote-control car, and it was actually controlled by scientists on Earth. Sojourner sent back photographs and provided information about the surface of Mars. Scientists are studying this information to learn more about the red planet.

Could We Live on Mars?

Some scientists talk of humans someday living on Mars. But if you're planning on becoming a Mars pioneer, be warned: Bring your own water. Most of the water there is trapped in icecaps at the planet's north and south poles.

People need the kind of atmosphere we have on Earth to survive. The air must contain oxygen. Also, it must be the right temperature—not too hot or too cold. If Mars had more oxygen in its air and if it were a little warmer, people might be able to live there.

Scientists are exploring ways to warm up the atmosphere on Mars and add oxygen to it. For example, they may be able to warm Mars with huge mirrors that reflect sunlight onto the planet. And adding oxygen would make the air on Mars breathable. If they could do these things, the atmosphere would change a lot. Then people would be able to breathe the air on Mars and go outside without wearing spacesuits.

Today, **NASA** scientists are studying ways to send people to Mars. Right now, it would take astronauts about a year to reach the red planet. The spaceship would have to be large enough to hold fuel, food, and other supplies for the crew. Visiting Mars may be our next big space adventure.

Many people like to imagine how we could live on Mars. This picture and the one on top of the opposite page show one artist's idea of what that life would be like.

This picture shows bands of clouds traveling around Jupiter. The oval-shaped Great Red Spot, *lower left,* is an enormous storm that drifts along one of the bands.

Jupiter, the Giant Planet

Jupiter is the biggest planet in our solar system. Just how big is it? It would take more than 1,000 Earths to fill up Jupiter.

Jupiter

Earth

Jupiter is the fifth planet from the sun. It has a small, rocky core, but most of it is surrounded by thick clouds of gas. The clouds form colored bands around the planet. Jupiter also has three thin rings of dust that sometimes look like one.

Wild windstorms are always raging in Jupiter's thick clouds. But can you imagine a huge hurricane that whirls for 300 years? Scientists believe that a hurricane on Jupiter called the Great Red Spot has been whirling for at least that long. This hurricane is more than three times as wide as Earth!

In 1979, two U.S. probes called Voyager 1 and Voyager 2 flew past Jupiter. Voyager 1 found one of Jupiter's rings, and Voyager 2 led to the discovery of three of the planet's moons. In December 1995, the U.S. space probe Galileo went into orbit around Jupiter.

Danger zone! Don't plan a vacation to Jupiter. You may get burned if you do. Jupiter sends out radiation so strong it can kill a human in just hours. Radiation is heat or light energy, like the kind sent out from the sun.

CAUTION
RADIATION AREA
KEEP OUT

Length of day: 10 hours, 39 minutes

Length of year: About 29 ½ earth-years

Number of moons: at least 18

Saturn and Its Famous Rings

Saturn, the sixth planet from the sun, is famous for its magnificent set of gleaming rings. Seven thin rings, made up of thousands of narrow ringlets, surround Saturn.

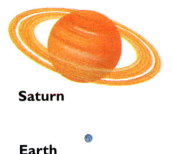

Saturn

Earth

Saturn's rings are formed of billions of pieces of ice, from tiny specks to very large "snowballs." These bits of ice travel around Saturn just as the moon travels around Earth.

Saturn is the second largest planet. It is nearly 10 times bigger than Earth. It has a rocky center, which is probably covered by a thin layer of liquid. And it is surrounded by thick layers of gas.

Big as it is, Saturn weighs less than a ball of water its size would weigh. If there were an ocean big enough to hold it, Saturn would float!

Scientists used the space probes Voyager 1 and Voyager 2 to study Saturn.

KNOW! It All!

Hold onto your hat! The strongest winds in the solar system blow around Saturn. They reach speeds about eight times stronger than a fierce hurricane on Earth.

Length of day:
17 hours, 8 minutes

Length of year:
84 earth-years

Number of moons:
15

Uranus, the Tilting Planet

Uranus

Earth

In England, in 1781, an amateur astronomer named William Herschel looked through a homemade **telescope** he set up in his garden. He found a new planet, Uranus, which became the first planet to be discovered by using a telescope.

Uranus is the seventh planet from the sun. It is a blue-green planet nearly four times wider than Earth. Scientists believe that Uranus has a rocky core covered by a deep ocean and thick clouds of gas. Uranus has 15 moons and at least 11 rings.

When Earth spins around its imaginary line called an **axis**, it is tilted like a spinning top. But the axis of Uranus is tilted even more than that—more than any other planet. At times, Uranus's north pole is pointed almost straight toward the sun. About 42 earth-years later, it is pointed away from the sun. Scientists learned much about Uranus from Voyager 2, which flew past the planet in 1986.

KNOW It All!!

Compared to the ocean on Uranus, Earth's ocean seems like a shallow swimming hole. But don't grab your towel and sunscreen just yet. At 4,000 °F (2,200 °C), the water and ammonia that make up Uranus's ocean would boil you in an instant!

Neptune

Earth

Neptune, a Distant Planet

Neptune is the eighth planet from the sun. It is about the same size as Uranus and is also about four times as wide as Earth. The planet is mostly made up of gases, but Neptune's center may be a mixture of slush and rocks.

Scientists are still learning about Neptune. Before 1989, it was thought that Neptune had only two moons. But that year the U.S. space probe Voyager 2 flew past and discovered six smaller, dark moons. Triton, one of Neptune's moons, has volcanoes that once gave off gases and slushy ice. Voyager 2 also discovered a ring system with three major bands.

KNOW It All!

Uranus helped scientists discover Neptune. As Uranus travels around the sun, it slows down at certain points. Scientists realized that what slows Uranus down is the gravity of another planet pulling on it. They began to look for that other planet and found Neptune!

Length of day:
16 hours, 7 minutes

Length of year:
About 165
earth-years

Number of moons:
8

Length of day:
About 6 earth-days

Length of year:
About 248
earth-years

Number of moons:
one

Pluto, the Mysterious Planet

Scientists do not know much about this planet. Pluto is so far away that it cannot be seen with a telescope. We know it is the ninth planet from the sun. And we know it is made up of frozen gases. Scientists estimate that its **diameter** is less than one-fifth the size of Earth.

Pluto is usually the farthest planet from the sun, but sometimes Neptune is actually farther! From outer space, looking down on the **solar system**, the orbits of most planets are almost perfect circles. Pluto's orbit looks less circular and more oval than the orbits of the other planets. At times, Pluto comes closer to the sun than Neptune.

Pluto

Earth

A moonlight walk on Pluto would be quite a sight. Charon, Pluto's moon, measures more than one-half the size of Pluto!

The painting on the opposite page shows what the moon Charon might look like from Pluto's surface. The inset photo shows how big Charon is compared to Pluto.

How Did the Planets Get Their Names?

Pluto
Pluto, the farthest planet in our solar system, was named after the Roman god of the dead.

Earth
Earth gets its name from an Old English word, *eorthe*, which means "land."

Neptune
Neptune was named after the Roman god of the sea.

Uranus
Uranus was named after an ancient sky god.

Venus
Venus was named after the Roman goddess of love and beauty because it is so beautiful to look at.

Jupiter
Jupiter, the biggest planet, was named after the most important Roman god.

Saturn
Saturn is named after the Roman god of farming.

Mars
Mars, the red planet, was named after the Romans' god of war, because war is bloody and blood is red.

Mercury
Seen from Earth, the planet Mercury appears, disappears, and appears again. And that is why it was named after the Roman god Mercury. As messenger of the gods, Mercury was thought to move swiftly back and forth between heaven and Earth.

A Space Mobile!

Make a model of the planets and the sun.

You Will Need:

4 dowel rods:
  one 17 inches (43 cm)
  one 21 inches (53 cm)
  one 35 inches (89 cm)
  one 43 inches (109 cm)

a spool of "invisible" nylon thread or fish line

4 curtain rings, 3/4 inch (2 cm) in diameter

a large piece of white posterboard

a compass

scissors

glue

crayons or markers

tape

a hole punch

a yardstick

a large paper plate

a small hook for ceiling

What To Do:

1. Measure and mark the longer and shorter rods as shown. Cross the two longer dowel rods. Tie them together with nylon thread. Do the same

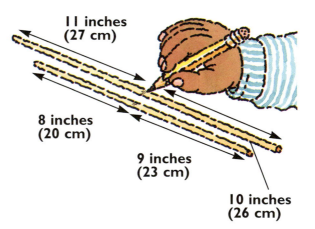

11 inches (27 cm)

8 inches (20 cm)

9 inches (23 cm)

10 inches (26 cm)

thing with the two shorter rods. Tie a ring above and below the points where the rods cross on each pair of rods.

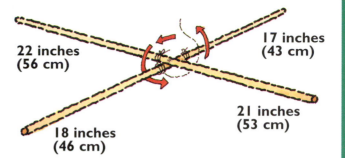

22 inches (56 cm)

17 inches (43 cm)

21 inches (53 cm)

18 inches (46 cm)

2. Cut 12 pieces of nylon thread and attach them to the rods as shown. Hang the mobile on a hook from the longer thread.

32 inches (81 cm)

16 in.

6 inches (15 cm)

16 in.

16 in.

16 in.

16 in.

16 in.

16 inches (41 cm)

16 in.

16 in.

3. Now you are ready to make the planets and the sun. Using a compass, draw 11 circles on the posterboard of the following sizes:

Sun, 4 1/2 in. (11.5 cm)
Jupiter, 3 3/4 in. (9.5 cm)
Saturn, 3 1/4 in. (8.5 cm)
Neptune, 2 1/2 in. (6.5 cm)
Uranus, 2 1/4 in. (6 cm)
Earth, 1 1/2 in. (4 cm)
Venus, 1 1/4 in. (3.5 cm)
Mars, 1 1/8 in. (3 cm)
Mercury, 1 in. (2.5 cm) make 2
Pluto, 3/4 in. (2 cm)

Cut out and label each circle. Glue the two Mercurys back to back.

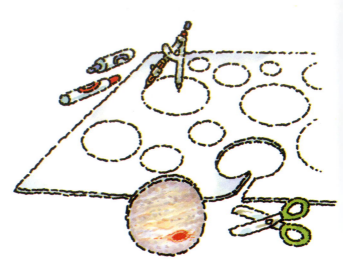

4. Color both sides of your sun and the planets. Look back at the descriptions and photos of the planets in this book for help.

5. Use the large paper plate for Saturn's magnificent set of gleaming rings. Color just the outer edge of the plate and cut a long slit in the middle of it. Slip the Saturn model through the slit and tape it in place.

6. Punch a hole near the top of the sun and each planet. Tie the sun to the center piece of thread. Tie the planets to the mobile. Mercury, the planet closest to the sun, should hang from the shortest section of the rod, Venus from the next shortest section, and so on. Look at the finished mobile shown below for help.

Now you can hang our solar system anywhere you like!

Neptune

Jupiter

Mars

Venus

Pluto

Saturn

Earth   Uranus

Mercury

Sun

Asteroids

Just as there are giant planets in the sun's family, there are also tiny planetlike objects. These small objects are called asteroids.

Most asteroids circle the sun in a ring between Mars and Jupiter. There are thousands of them. Most are less than 1 mile (1.6 kilometers) across, but some are several hundred miles across. The largest asteroid, named Ceres (SIHR eez), is about 600 miles (970 kilometers) wide, much bigger than the moons of Mars.

The larger asteroids are nearly ball-shaped, like the bigger planets. The smaller asteroids are bumpy and jagged.

Asteroids often bump into one another and break into smaller bits. Sometimes they are knocked out of their orbits and begin traveling in another direction. These asteroids become meteoroids that sometimes collide with other planets. **Collisions** like this made craters on Mars, Mercury, and Earth's moon. Bits of asteroids also become meteors, the "shooting stars" that we see from Earth.

An asteroid could collide with a planet.

The Stars

Stars are huge balls of glowing gas in the sky. The sun is the only star close enough to Earth to look like a large ball to us. The other stars are so far away that they look like tiny dots of light.

What Are Stars?

Stars may look close, but they are actually very far away—much farther from Earth than the planets are. The nearest **star** to us, after the sun, is so far away that it takes more than four years for its light to reach us! Some stars are so

Why do stars twinkle? They don't. But their light is bent several times by layers of moving air in our atmosphere. The bending of a star's light makes it look like the star is twinkling.

People always have gazed at the stars. Whether for hobby or science, **telescopes** help bring the stars into sharper focus so we can learn more about them.

far away that their light takes billions of years to reach us. That twinkle of light you see in the sky tonight may have been given off before Earth existed!

How many stars are there? Scientists believe that there are about 10 billion trillion stars in the universe. To understand how large a number this is, imagine that all the people in the world had to count an equal number of stars one by one. Each person would have to count more than 1 1/2 trillion stars. And, even if you could count 1,000 stars per second for 24 hours a day, you would need 50 years to count 1 1/2 trillion stars!

Where do stars go during the day? They don't go anywhere. Our daytime sky is so bright, we just can't see them.

Meteoroids, the Shooting Stars

If you ever wished on a shooting star, you were really wishing on a burning rock. Sometimes a big lump of rock and metal called a **meteoroid** zooms through the blackness of space. For billions of years, this meteoroid has been zipping around and around the sun. But now it is heading straight for Earth.

The lump of rock enters Earth's **atmosphere**. It is traveling so fast that Earth's air rubs hard against it. This makes the meteoroid very hot.

Bits of the rock burn up, leaving a trail of glowing gas. Seen from Earth, it looks like a bright streak flashing across the sky. Some people call the streak a "shooting star" or a "falling star."

As many as 200 million meteoroids come into Earth's atmosphere every day! Most of them are small and burn up completely. But if a meteoroid is big enough, it may not burn up before it hits the ground. Instead, it may come smashing to Earth and make a crater— a big hole in the ground.

KNOW It All!

Stars come in different colors— red, orange, yellow, white, and blue. A star's color tells us how hot it is. The hottest stars shine with a brilliant blue light. White stars are the next hottest. Yellow stars, such as our sun, are cooler, and red stars are the coolest of all.

A "Star" with a Tail

For thousands of years, whenever a bright star with a glowing tail appeared in the sky, people were afraid. If it seemed to grow bigger and brighter, some people thought the end of the world was near! Now we know that these "stars" are actually just **comets**.

Billions of comets travel around and around the sun. Most are balls of frozen **gas**, like snowballs mixed with dust. They come from two groups of comets near the edge of the **solar system**. Just beyond Pluto, usually the farthest planet, is the group called the Kuiper (KOY puhr) belt. Beyond that lies the ball-shaped Oort cloud.

At first, comets have no tails. But when a comet gets near the sun, the sun's heat melts some of the frozen gas. Gas and dust stream off into space, forming a tail. The tail glows because sunlight shines on the gas and dust and also releases energy from the gas.

The center of a comet's icy head may be several miles wide. It is surrounded by a cloud of gas as much as one million miles (1,600,000 kilometers) wide. Its tail may be millions of miles long.

tail

head

KNOW It All!

A comet travels around the sun in a stretched-out orbit called an ellipse. The solar wind from the sun blows particles from the comet into a tail that always points away from the sun.

Halley's Comet

The comet we call Halley's Comet was first seen more than 2,000 years ago. It was sighted by Chinese **astronomers** in 240 B.C. It appeared again and again over the centuries, but most people did not realize it was the same comet. They believed that comets appeared by chance and traveled through space in no set path.

An English astronomer named Edmund Halley proved them wrong. He discovered that the comet traveled in a set path around the sun.

Halley knew that the paths of comets seen in 1531 and 1607 were exactly the same as the path of a comet observed in 1682. And he realized that these were all the same comet! Halley also noted that 76 years had passed between 1531 and 1607. And between 1607 and 1682, 75 years had passed. He predicted that people would see that comet again 76 years later and at fairly regular intervals after that.

Halley's Comet appears about every 76 years.

Sure enough, the comet was sighted on Christmas Day in 1758. Halley's Comet became the most famous comet in history.

Halley's Comet as seen from a desert in the United States

Star Pictures

If you look up at the sky at night, you might imagine pictures or shapes in the stars. Long ago, people used their imaginations to find star pictures, too. To some people, one group of stars looked like a hunter carrying a club and holding the pelt of an animal he had killed. Other star groups looked like a crab, a bull's head, and even a dragon! People named star groups after the pictures they made.

Today, amateur astronomers still use these star pictures, called **constellations**, to find the stars they want to study.

Draco

108

The star picture called the Big Dipper is toward the left of this photo. Can you find the similarly shaped Little Dipper to the right?

Star Stories

In ancient times, when people found pictures in the stars, they made up stories to go along with the pictures. People of different cultures sometimes had different stories about the same group of stars. Here are just a few of those stories.

Scorpio

The ancient Polynesians told a story of stars that were born in a canoe. Scorpio is the tail of the canoe. A story from Australia says Scorpio is a crocodile, an opossum, and a water bird.

Scorpio

Cancer

Ancient Greeks tell a story that the goddess Hera was angry with Hercules, the son of the sky god, Zeus. While Hercules was fighting with a monster, she sent Cancer the crab to distract him. The crab was crushed by Hercules's foot. Hera rewarded the crab by placing it among the stars.

Cancer

Gemini

Ancient Greeks said that twin brothers, Castor and Pollux, were the constellation Gemini. A story from northwest Siberia tells of two elks running away from two hunters. The twins of Gemini are the two elks.

The Indians of Mato Grosso, Brazil, told a different story. The sun gave three flutes to men and taught them to play tunes and dance. Gemini is one of the flutes.

Gemini

Cygnus

For thousands of years, many groups of people have seen this constellation as a bird. According to one story, the Greek god Zeus turned himself into a swan to become attractive to a woman. The Aleut people of Alaska tell about a man who set off to hunt seal in a kayak. The hunter dips his oar into the freezing water. Cygnus is the kayak, the oar, and the seal hunter.

Cygnus

Orion, the Hunter

There are many stories about Orion, called the Giant by Arabs and the mummy of Osiris by ancient Egyptians. To ancient Greeks, Orion was a giant and great hunter turned into stars by the gods. Three bright stars in the constellation represent Orion's belt, and five fainter stars below the belt are his sword.

An Australian story tells of three fishermen who make up the constellation Orion. A story from central India tells of the Sing-Bonga. The Sing-Bonga went to the heavenly blacksmith. The blacksmith made an iron plow. The sword and belt of Orion are the plow. Auriga, a nearby constellation, is the blacksmith, the bellows, and the fire.

Orion

Ursa Major, the Great Bear

The Micmac people of North America tell a story about a great bear that wakes from a long sleep in late spring. He is chased by seven birds. In summer, the birds chase the bear across the northern horizon. In fall, one of the birds strikes the bear with an arrow. The bear falls on its back. Blood drips down to Earth and paints the leaves red. In winter, the bear's spirit enters another bear. The next spring, that bear gets chased across the sky.

In the United States and Canada, the seven brightest stars of Ursa Major are called the Big Dipper. The Chinese believe that those seven stars form a bushel measure used to bring food to people during a famine. In India, the seven stars represent seven ancient sages, or wise people.

Ursa Major

The Sia Indians of South America tell about a giant beetle who was given a sack of stars to carry from the underworld to the world above. The beetle was told not to open the sack, but he did. All the stars scattered across the sky. A few stars were left in the sack and these were used to make patterns in the sky. We call these patterns Ursa Major, Pleiades, and Orion's Belt.

If you live in
the Northern
Hemisphere, use
the star chart on
page 115.

Finding Star Pictures

If you live in the Northern **Hemisphere**, you will be able to see the constellations shown on the star chart on page 115 during most of the year. If you live in the Southern Hemisphere, you will be able to see the constellations shown on the star chart on page 117 during most of the year. And if you live in the southern United States, Hawaii, northern Australia, or somewhere else close to the equator, you will sometimes be able to see some of the constellations on both charts.

On the charts, stars in each constellation are joined with lines that show the constellation's shape. To use the charts, take this book outdoors at about 9 o'clock on a clear, moonless night. If you live in

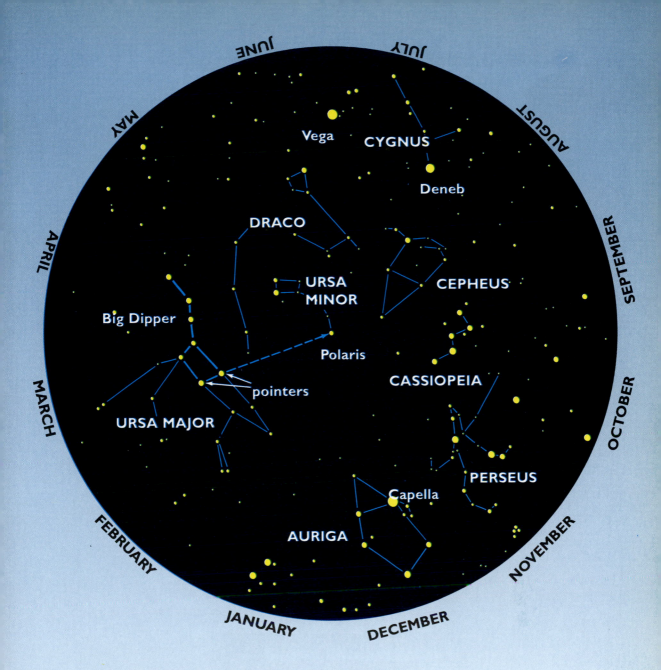

the Northern Hemisphere, face south.
If you live in the Southern Hemisphere,
face north.

You will need a flashlight to see the chart,
but be sure to cover the light with red
cellophane. Otherwise, it will be hard to see
the stars when you look up at the sky.

If you live in the Southern Hemisphere, use the star chart on page 117.

The constellations move into a different part of the sky each month. The names of the months are given around the outside of each chart. Hold the book so that the name of the present month is closest to your chest. The chart will then show where the constellations are when you look up at the sky.

On the charts, each constellation has a Latin name. Some of the names are based on what ancient people thought the constellations looked like. For example, in the Northern Hemisphere, there is a constellation called Draco, which means "dragon." In the Southern Hemisphere, there is a constellation called Crux, which means "cross." The charts also show a few of the brightest stars, such as Vega and Canopus.

If you live in or near a city, you may not be able to see all of the stars or constellations because of the city lights. But you will nearly always be able to see the brightest stars on cloudless nights.

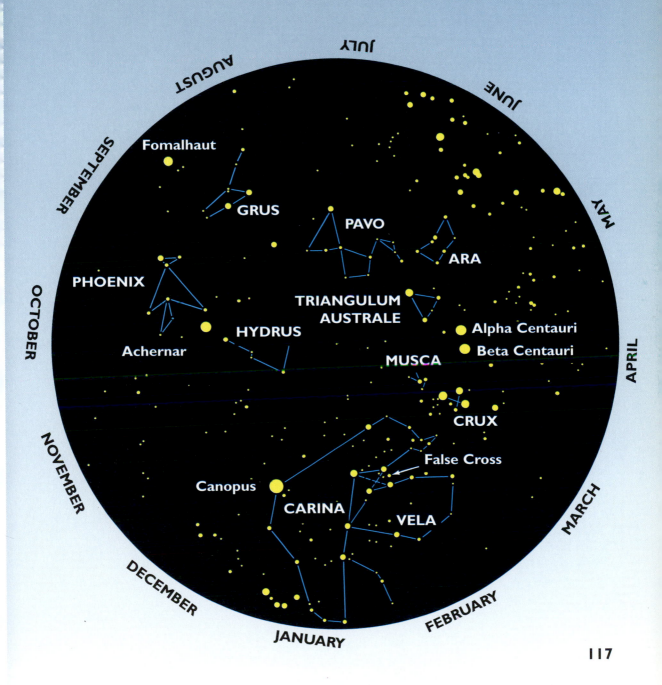

Exploding Stars

In the year 1054, a very bright star suddenly appeared in the sky. It was so bright that it could be seen in the daytime. Then it slowly began to fade away. After a time, it disappeared. What kind of star was this?

The disappearing star was a star that had exploded. Certain kinds of stars can explode. A small star called a **white dwarf** may suddenly flare up and become much brighter. Such a star is called a **nova** (NOH vuh). After a time, the brightness fades away.

When a very large star called a supergiant begins to die, it explodes, too. This explosion sends a gigantic cloud of glowing gas out into space. This kind of explosion is called a **supernova**.

A star that becomes a supernova may become a billion times brighter. The bright star seen in the sky in 1054 was a supernova.

Not all stars are the same size. The stars called giant stars may be a hundred times bigger than our sun. And supergiant stars may be a thousand times bigger! The smallest stars are called dwarf stars. The sun is a yellow dwarf. Some dwarf stars are smaller than our Earth. In fact, some dwarf stars would cover only the continent of Asia.

Misty Shapes in Space

In space, between the stars, there are big patches of gas or dust, or both. These are called nebulas (NEHB yuh luhs).

There are four kinds of nebulas. One kind seems to glow because it reflects the light from nearby stars. This kind of nebula is made of gas and dust and is called a reflective (rih FLEHK tihv) nebula.

Horsehead Nebula, a dark nebula in Orion

Other nebulas are collections of dust, gas, and special gases that give off their own light. They are called emissions (ee MIHSH uhnz) nebulas.

Other nebulas are collections of cloudy dust and gas that often block the stars behind them or make these stars difficult to see. These are called dark nebulas.

Planetary (PLAN uh tair ee) nebulas are mostly ring-shaped. They are shells of gas that usually surround a star that has exploded.

The Geat Nebula, an emissions nebula in Orion

Witchhead Nebula, a reflective nebula

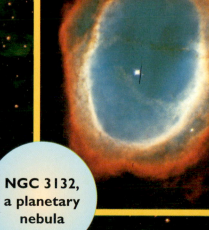

NGC 3132, a planetary nebula

Star Twins

Many stars seem to come in pairs, like twins. Some stars even come in triplets and quadruplets.

These twin or triplet stars were formed at the same time, but they are often very different.

Sometimes a giant orange star is twinned with a medium-sized blue star. Sometimes a yellow star, like our sun, is matched with a white dwarf star.

Twin stars affect each other. If one star is heavier than the other, the lighter one will orbit the heavier one. If they are about the same weight, they will orbit the same point in the sky.

Such twin stars are often so close together, and so far from Earth, that they look like a single, twinkling star. Only with special instruments and telescopes can we tell that there is more than one star.

Black Holes

In space there are stars in which **gravity** is so strong that nothing can escape from it—not even light. We call these stars **black holes**. The gravity of black holes is so strong that it pulls in nearby stars, drawing them toward it.

Astronomers believe that a black hole forms when a massive star runs out of

energy and is crushed by its own gravity. A star that runs out of energy collapses and then explodes. The exploding star throws off its outer layers, but the remaining core continues to collapse and becomes a black hole.

Because black holes are invisible, they are hard for scientists to find. However, most astronomers believe our **galaxy** contains millions of them. Astronomers have found strong evidence for seven black holes in our galaxy and in a nearby galaxy.

The Shapes of Galaxies

A galaxy consists of stars, dust, and gas held together by gravity. Small galaxies have fewer than a billion stars. Astronomers have photographed millions of galaxies through telescopes. They believe there are about 100 billion galaxies in the **universe**. Each galaxy may hold billions of stars.

Galaxies come in many different shapes and sizes. However, there are four main shapes that we can recognize in the sky They are shown on these pages.

a barred spiral galaxy

a spiral galaxy

an elliptical galaxy

A spiral galaxy looks like a giant whirlpool of stars with a flattened ball in the middle. Out of this ball come two or more spiral-shaped arms of stars. Our galaxy, the **Milky Way,** is a spiral galaxy.

A barred spiral galaxy has a sausage shape in the middle. From the ends of the sausage come two spiral arms of stars.

Elliptical galaxies are curved. Some are almost round. Others look like flattened balls or footballs.

Irregular galaxies do not seem to have any special shape. Some look like messy spirals. The Magellanic Clouds, the closest galaxies to ours, are irregular galaxies.

an irregular galaxy

Many galaxies are grouped together in space. Such groups are called clusters (KLUHS tuhrs) of galaxies. Some galaxies stand alone between the clusters.

127

The glowing cloud we call the Milky Way is made up of billions of stars that are trillions of miles apart.

The Milky Way

The Milky Way is the name of the spiral galaxy in which we live. It is made up of hundreds of billions of stars, including our sun.

The Milky Way looks like a gigantic cloud of stars, all very close together. But

the distance between any two
Milky Way stars varies.
Just as Earth moves
around the sun, the sun
and the other stars
move around the
center of the galaxy.
The galaxy is so big, and
our sun is so far from its
center, that it takes the sun
more than 250 million years to
go all the way around.

Our sun is part of a gigantic cloud of
stars called the Milky Way Galaxy.

sun

This photograph of the Andromeda Galaxy was taken through a telescope.

Our Galaxy Neighbors

We live in the Milky Way Galaxy, but there are many other galaxies in the universe. Most of them are so far away that we can't see them without a telescope. But there are three galaxies that we can see with just our eyes.

One of these is the **Andromeda Galaxy**. It is bigger than our own Milky Way Galaxy and contains more than 150 billion stars.

The other two galaxies we can see without a telescope are the Large and Small Magellanic Clouds. They can both be seen from the Southern Hemisphere.

The Magellanic Clouds, the Andromeda Galaxy, and our galaxy, along with others, form a group of about 30 galaxies called the Local Group. Beyond the Local Group lies a whole universe of galaxies!

This galaxy is called the Large Magellanic Cloud.

Here is an artist's idea of what the Local Group of galaxies looks like.

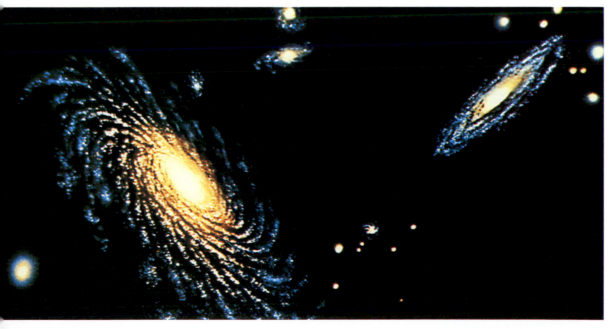

Quasars

Out in space there are extremely bright objects that we call **quasars** (KWAY zahrz). Most quasars are about the size of the solar system. But they can be a trillion times brighter than the sun.

The word *quasar* is short for "quasi-stellar radio source," which is an object that looks like a star but is not really a star.

In photos of space, quasars look like stars. But we can tell that they are giving off as much light and heat as 100,000 Milky Way galaxies!

Quasars are traveling away from us very fast. And they are very far away. They are so far from us, we do not see them as they are now. We see them as they were about 15 billion years ago. Astronomers study them to find out what the universe was like so long ago.

Where do quasars get all their energy? Many astronomers believe that quasars have massive black holes at their centers. Energy comes from matter swirling in toward the black hole.

Waves from Space

Right this minute, you are being hit by waves from outer space. These are radiation waves, and space is full of them.

Radiation (RAY dee AY shuhn) is the giving off of a certain type of energy. This type of energy is given off by most things in space, including the sun and other stars, planets, and the huge clouds of gas and dust called nebulas.

All life on Earth depends on the radiation given off by the sun. The sun's energy provides heat and light. The heat warms Earth. Its light provides food for plants, which in turn feed animals and people.

Radiation waves travel incredibly fast, almost as fast as light. When radiation strikes an object, it may give some or all of its energy to the object. When radiation waves hit you, you

Pulsars (PUHL sahrz) are very small stars whose **radio waves** sweep over Earth in bursts, or pulses. The time between pulses ranges from a fraction of a second to almost four seconds. The time between the pulses is short because the pulsars are spinning very fast.

can't feel them because they are made of such tiny bits of matter. Earth's atmosphere shuts out some radiation. Scientists think there is also a kind of "wall" in our solar system that stops other radiation waves as well. This is a good thing, because too much radiation can make people sick.

KNOW It All!

Long ago there lived a people called the Vikings. These fierce sailors traveled in big ships. But when storms threw them off course, the Vikings weren't lost for long. They looked for a star they called the lodestar to guide them. Most scholars believe that the Vikings' lodestar was what we call the **North Star**. The North Star does not move very much. It will almost always be straight north.

Light Show in the Sky

People who live far enough north or far enough south often see a light show called an aurora (uh RAWR uh) on clear nights. Great sheets of colorful light seem to ripple in the sky like curtains in a breeze.

This light show takes place in Earth's atmosphere, but it is caused by the sun. The sun shoots particles of matter into space. Many of these particles come to Earth. Near Earth's North and South poles are two points that act like giant magnets. These points are called the north and south magnetic poles. These two magnets attract the particles of energy from the sun. When these particles collide with other particles in Earth's atmosphere, they glow. They fill the sky with shimmering light.

aurora borealis

Studying the Universe

Since ancient times, people have studied heavenly bodies. Astronomers of the past knew only about the objects they could see with just their eyes or with basic telescopes. Today, astronomers have powerful telescopes, computers, and many other tools to help them learn about the universe.

Early Skywatchers

In ancient times, most people had no way of knowing what was beyond the farthest mountain they could see. To help explain what the world looked like, they made up stories.

One ancient Eastern legend said that the world was flat and rested on the backs of four elephants. The elephants all stood on a huge tortoise, and the tortoise stood on an even bigger serpent. And the serpent? He floated on the surface of an endless ocean.

In ancient India, people believed Earth was a flat disk surrounded by an ocean. A layer above Earth held the clouds. The sky formed another layer above the clouds. The heavenly bodies moved around the sky in chariots drawn by horses. A huge dome-shaped shell surrounded and protected all three layers.

The ancient Egyptians believed in a sky goddess named Nut. Nut, it was said, supported the heavens on her back.

To the ancient Navajo, who lived in a hot dry desert, the rainbow was a god. The sky was their father who watched over them.

In the Navajo world, the rainbow god arches above Earth as Big Wind and Big Thunder watch over the sky beyond.

Around the Sun

Many years ago, people thought the **moon**, sun, **planets**, and even the **stars** all revolved around Earth! But in the 1500's, a Polish **astronomer** named Nicolaus (nihk uh LAY uhs) Copernicus (kuh PUR nuh kuhs) taught people that the sun was in the center of the **solar system**. He said that all the planets, including Earth, moved around the sun.

This is a simple plan of people's idea of the solar system before Copernicus.

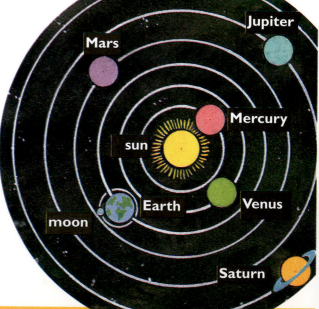

This is a simple plan of Copernicus's idea of the solar system. During Copernicus's time, Saturn was the most distant planet discovered.

Kepler found that planets move in ellipses, or ovals, around the sun.

a short ellipse

a long ellipse

Copernicus was right about that, but he was not quite right about the paths the planets took. Copernicus thought each planet moved in a circular **orbit** around the sun. Another astronomer, Johannes (yoh HAHN uhs) Kepler, discovered that the planets moved around the sun in **ellipses**, or ovals, not in circles.

Kepler said that a planet is closer to the sun at certain times. He discovered that the planets move faster when they are closer to the sun and slower when they are farther away from it. He also learned that the planets closest to the sun move faster than the others.

KNOW It All!

On what planet would somebody get to have the most birthdays? Which planet is closest to the sun? The answer to both questions is Mercury, where a year is shorter than on any other planet!

The First Telescopes

The first **telescope** was probably invented in 1608 by a Dutch eyeglass maker named Hans Lippershey. He made his telescope by putting two lenses with slightly different shapes at opposite ends of a tube. The following year, after hearing about Lippershey's invention, an Italian scientist named Galileo (gal uh LAY oh) made his own telescope.

Galileo

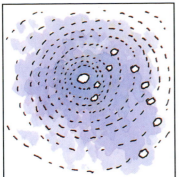

Galileo, like Copernicus, believed the planets went around the sun.

He looked at Venus for many months. At first, it was a small, round disk.

Over time, its position and shape changed.

Slowly, from night to night, the disk darkened into a half circle.

At the same time, it grew bigger.

Soon, the half circle had changed into a slender crescent.

Galileo was one of the first people to use the telescope to look at objects in the sky. He made many important discoveries, such as the craters on the moon and the spots on the sun.

Galileo discovered four of Jupiter's moons and learned that they went around the planet. He was the first to notice that Venus had phases, very much like our moon. He also discovered that the Milky Way Galaxy consisted of many stars.

label: lens

How Telescopes Work

Telescopes make distant objects look bigger. Two main types of telescopes are refracting telescopes and reflecting telescopes.

A refracting (rih FRAK tihng) telescope gathers light from a distant object and focuses it through two lenses. It has one big lens in front and a smaller lens you look through. The lens at the front usually has a bulge on both sides. It is thick in the middle and thin around the edges. This lens collects the light from a distant planet or star and forms an image of it in the telescope tube. The other lens, the eyepiece, is like a very powerful magnifying glass. It makes things look much bigger.

Refracting telescope
The arrows show the path of light rays as they travel down a refracting telescope.

label: eyepiece

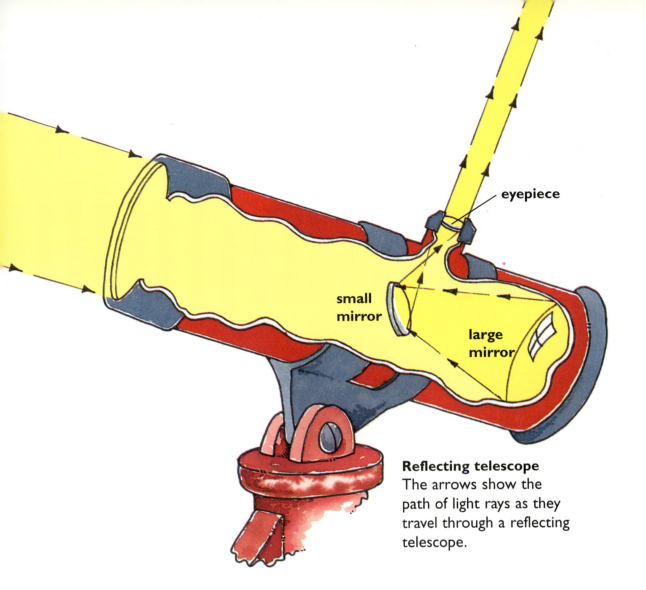

eyepiece

small
mirror

large
mirror

Reflecting telescope
The arrows show the
path of light rays as they
travel through a reflecting
telescope.

A reflecting (rih FLEHK tihng)
telescope uses a large mirror to collect
the light, instead of a lens. The mirror is
at the bottom end of the tube. The light
from a star goes straight down the tube
and strikes the mirror. Then the light is
reflected up the tube. A smaller mirror
reflects the collected light. The light
comes out through a hole in the side of
the tube, where the eyepiece is.

Tabletop Telescope

You can look at the night sky with a simple telescope you make yourself. Here's how.

What To Do:

1. Place the magnifying mirror near a window to reflect the moon or stars. The mirror should stand at an angle to the window so that the light is reflected onto the window or the wall next to it.

2. Prop up the flat mirror between the magnifying mirror and the window or wall, in the path of the reflected light. From behind the magnifying mirror, you should see the reflected light from the moon or the stars in the flat mirror. You may need to adjust the position of both mirrors to get a good reflection of the moon or a group of stars. Every few minutes you will have to readjust the mirrors because of the motion of the moon and stars.

3. Use your magnifying glass to examine the reflection that appears in the flat mirror. Move the magnifying glass back and forth until you see the reflection clearly.

How well your telescope works depends on the quality of your magnifying glass and on finding the right distance and positions between the mirrors.

This astronomer is adjusting the telescope in an observatory dome.

This observatory was built at La Palma on the Canary Islands because the air there is very clear.

Houses for Telescopes

Observatories are like houses for telescopes. Some observatories have cameras and other machines that record the information gathered by telescopes.

Most observatories are easy to spot. Many of them have a dome that looks like an upside-down bowl. The dome keeps the telescope safe from bad weather.

Each dome has a slit through which the telescope can be pointed toward the sky. When the telescope is not being used, this slit is covered by a shutter or a metal blind.

Since the telescope is used to look at different parts of the sky, the astronomers must be able to point the slit in any direction. The dome has wheels at its bottom edge. These wheels run on a circular track near the top of the observatory building. So, the whole dome can be turned.

Most big observatories are built far away from the lights of big cities. City air has dust and smoke that bend light back to Earth. This makes the sky glow, so it is harder to see the stars clearly.

This observatory was used long ago in Yucatán, Mexico.

Watching the Stars Move

It's the middle of the day. The lights around you fade. Soon, all you can see are faint stars glimmering overhead. Slowly, the moon rises above the horizon and moves across the sky. But how can you see all this in the middle of the day? It's easy. You're in a planetarium (plan uh TAIR ee uhm).

A planetarium is like a special movie theater. Instead of showing movies on a flat screen, the projector in a planetarium shows pictures of planets, stars, and moons on a domed ceiling. Your chair tilts toward the dome. Stars and planets seem to move across the sky. They can move faster than in real life because the projector controls them. In just a few minutes you can see how the stars and planets move across the sky all night. You can even see the movement of stars through a season or a year.

Planetarium at Home

Here's how to make a simple planetarium projector.

You Will Need:

an empty oatmeal container
  with plastic lid
scissors
construction paper
tracing paper
a pencil
a paper hole puncher
a flashlight

What To Do:

1. Have an adult cut out the bottom of an oatmeal box and the center of the lid.

2. Trace the outside of the lid on construction paper. Cut out the circle just inside the line so that it fits inside the lid.

Step 2

154

3. Using the tracing paper, trace this constellation.

Step 3

The Lion

4. Place the tracing over the construction paper. Use a pencil or hole-punch to make the holes for the stars.

Step 4

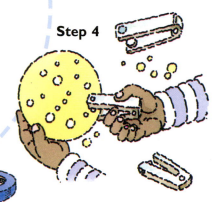

Step 5

5. Fit the construction paper circle inside the lid. Place the lid on the box.

6. In a dark room, hold the box over a flashlight. Look up. You should see the constellation on the ceiling. You have made a planetarium!

Step 6

Find constellations in other books and trace them. Then make more construction paper constellations. Now you can stargaze any day, even when it rains. But on clear nights, go out and look at the real stars in the sky!

Great Astronomers

Who were some great astronomers in history?

Isaac Newton

In the 1600's, **Isaac Newton,** an English scientist, figured out the rules for the movement of the stars and the planets. He also realized that the planets move as they do because of the force of gravity between the planets and the sun. In addition, Newton made a new kind of telescope. Instead of using two lenses, he used a curved mirror and a small lens. Most of the huge telescopes used today are based on Newton's.

William Herschel, who was born in Germany and moved to England, discovered the planet Uranus in 1781. He did so with a telescope he invented. His telescope was 4 feet (1.2 meters) wide, the largest telescope until 1845. Herschel was also one of the first modern astronomers to study the Milky Way Galaxy.

Herschel's telescope

Friedrich Wilhelm Bessel

In the early 1800's, German astronomer **Friedrich Wilhelm Bessel** explained why stars seem to move in the sky.

In the late 1800's, **Annie Jump Cannon,** the leading American female astronomer of her time, discovered 300 stars that change their brightness.

Annie Jump Cannon

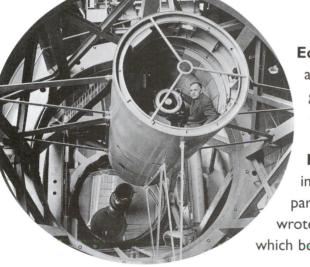

Edwin Hubble, an American astronomer, discovered in 1929 that galaxies are moving away from each other at very high speeds.

In the late 1990's, **Stephen Hawking,** a British scientist, made important discoveries about gravity, particularly black holes. He also wrote several important books, one of which became very popular.

Edwin Hubble sitting in the observer's cage inside the Hale telescope at Mount Palomar, California

Helen Sawyer Hogg, an American-born astronomer, began publishing works about ball-like groups of stars that vary in brightness. Sometimes, astronomers use information from Hogg's discoveries to figure out how far certain stars are from Earth.

Helen Sawyer Hogg

The First Rocket

On March 16, 1926, a strange metal contraption went roaring up into the sky. It climbed until it was only a speck. The world's first liquid-fuel **rocket** had just been **launched**.

That rocket was built by Dr. Robert H. Goddard, an American scientist. And he kept building better rockets through the 1920's and 1930's.

Another great rocket was invented by a German **engineer** named Wernher von Braun. Von Braun's team built the V-2 guided missile. Later von Braun came to the United States. His team built the rocket that launched the first successful U.S. **satellite**.

A Balloon Rocket

Launches are exciting to watch. Here's how you can launch a balloon.

What To Do:

1. Cut off about one-third of the straw. Then slide the short piece of straw about halfway into the neck of the balloon. With the string, tie the end of the balloon firmly around the straw. Make sure that the straw is not pinched shut.

2. Fold the paper in half lengthwise, then open it up. Poke a small hole in the middle of the creased line with the point of the pencil. Slide the paper over the end of the straw. This is the tail of your balloon rocket.

3. Blow up the balloon through the straw. Press your thumb over the end of the straw to keep the air in.

4. Now let go. The air will rush out of the balloon, making it shoot forward.

A real rocket works in a similar way. Burning fuels make gases that rush out of the rocket and propel it into outer space.

You Will Need:

a piece of thick paper that is about 2 by 4 inches (5 by 10 cm)

a drinking straw

a balloon

scissors

a pencil

string

A Manufactured Moon

You know that a moon is a natural object that orbits a body in **space**. But did you know that another name for a moon is *satellite?* An *artificial* (ahr tuh FIHSH uhl) moon, or satellite, is one made by people. Here's the story of the first **artificial satellite**.

On October 4, 1957, a rocket took off from Earth. It carried an artificial satellite that weighed 184 pounds (83 kilograms), and its powerful engine drove it at a speed of nearly 5 miles (8 kilometers) per second. The Soviet scientists who had launched it from the former Soviet Union watched nervously as it roared into space.

The rocket quickly reached a height at which it could begin to orbit. Then its nose was automatically pushed off, and a metal globe about the size of a basketball was hurled into space. The globe then went into orbit.

Four long, slim antennas (an TEHN uhz) automatically opened up out of the metal ball and began broadcasting. Scientists at

Sputnik was an artificial satellite that had antennas. The antennas sent signals back to Earth.

a special radio station on Earth began hearing a steady, high *beep-beep-beep*.

That signal told them that the globe was out in space, moving around Earth. Back on Earth, people were very excited. The first manufactured moon, or artificial satellite, had been launched. This artificial satellite became known as Sputnik, which is the Russian word for "traveler." It orbited Earth every 96 minutes.

Sometimes it was about 145 miles (230 kilometers) from Earth. At other parts of its orbit, it went about 585 miles (941 kilometers) from Earth.

Artificial Satellites

Earth observation satellite

communications satellite

navigation satellite

Artificial satellites send signals. There are many different kinds of signals they send. Each carries a different type of information.

Some artificial satellites send their signals to radios, beepers, and television sets. These are called communications satellites. Ships, aircraft, and even some cars use navigation satellites to figure out their location on Earth. Weather satellites take pictures of the movements of the clouds. Scientific research satellites send information about the universe. Scientists can use an earth observation satellite to look at Earth and find heavily polluted areas or damaged forests. Military satellites can send signals about the movement of missiles, ships, and soldiers.

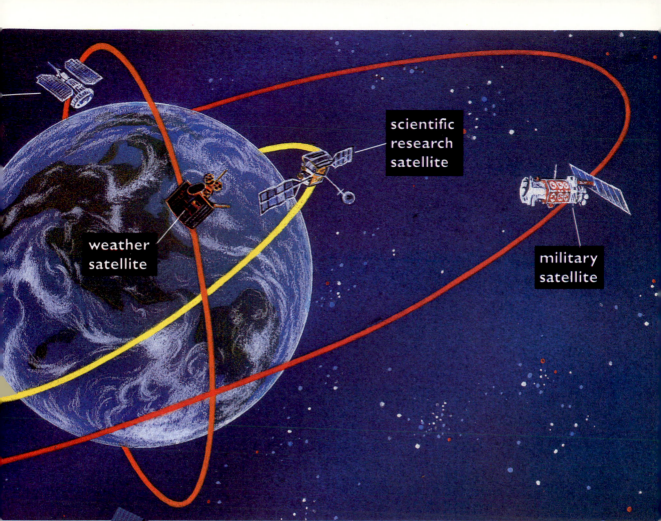

scientific
research
satellite

weather
satellite

military
satellite

solar panel

solar panel

The solar panels on an
artificial satellite collect
power from the sun to
make the satellite work.
Its antenna sends signals
to another satellite,
which sends them to
Earth.

antenna

People in Space

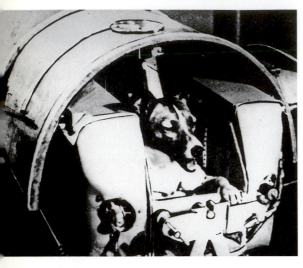

Laika

Many people have explored the sky from Earth. Others have traveled up there for a closer look.

The first space travelers from Earth were not people at all. They were animals! In November 1957, scientists from the Soviet Union sent a dog named Laika into space in a satellite called Sputnik 2. Laika's journey proved that animals could survive a trip into space.

On January 31, 1961, the United States sent Ham, a chimpanzee, into space in the Mercury space capsule. The animals' flights helped scientists prepare for the challenge of sending people into space!

Not long after Ham's journey, on April 12, 1961, Yuri Gagarin from the Soviet Union became the first person in orbit. His flight lasted 108 minutes.

Yuri Gagarin

John Glenn

Alan B. Shepard became the first U.S. **astronaut** launched into space. He took off May 5, 1961.

John Glenn became the first U.S. astronaut to orbit Earth. In 1962, he circled Earth three times.

Valentina Tereshkova

In 1963, **cosmonaut** Valentina Tereshkova became the first woman in space. She made 45 orbits of Earth.

The first **spacewalk** took place in 1965. That year Alexei A. Leonov, from the Soviet Union, became the first person to step outside a **spacecraft.**

In 1984, American astronaut Bruce McCandless attached himself to a jet-propelled backpack. This let him move around in space without a lifeline linked to his craft. McCandless was his own miniature spaceship! He kept his face toward the shuttle so that he wouldn't lose sight of it.

In 1991, Helen Sharman became Britain's first astronaut in space.

In 1992, Mae Carol Jemison became the first African American woman to travel in space.

Helen Sharman

Mae Carol Jemison

In 1995, cosmonaut Valery Polyakov completed a record 438 days in space. In 1996, American astronaut Shannon Lucid broke two records for time spent in space with 188 days. That was the longest time for any woman and the longest time for any American.

Valery Polyakov

First Person on the Moon

One of the greatest adventures in history took place on July 20, 1969. A human being visited Earth's closest neighbor in space. After a voyage of almost 240,000 miles (386,000 kilometers) across space, American astronaut Neil A. Armstrong became the first person to set foot on the moon.

Four days earlier, the spacecraft Apollo 11 had been launched. On board were Michael Collins, the pilot, and two astronauts, Edwin E. Aldrin, Jr., and Neil Armstrong.

On July 20, Apollo 11 reached the moon and circled it in orbit.

Armstrong and Aldrin entered the lunar module section of the spacecraft, called the Eagle, and separated it from Apollo 11. A blast of the Eagle's engine sent it speeding down toward the moon's surface.

There is no air on the moon, so the Eagle could not fly down like an airplane. It had to fall, at a speed of more than 2 miles (3 kilometers) per minute. Bursts from the engine slowed it down enough so that it landed gently. Apollo 11, with Collins on board, continued orbiting the moon.

That evening, Armstrong radioed to Earth, "The Eagle has landed." Armstrong descended the ladder first. As he set foot on the moon, he said, "That's one small step for a man, one giant leap for mankind." After collecting rocks and soil samples, the two men rocketed part of the Eagle back up to Apollo 11.

On the first visit to the moon, astronauts set up experiments. Some of the equipment they used is still there.

What Are Space Labs?

A Soviet Soyuz spacecraft, *rear*, prepares to dock with Salyut 1, the first space laboratory.

Some things can be done in space that can't be done on Earth. For example, certain materials won't mix on Earth because of gravity, but they will mix in space. This could make it possible to produce new kinds of metals, medicines, and other useful things in space.

So how can scientists test such materials? They can test them in a **laboratory** called a **space station**. A space station is a place where scientists and technicians can live and work in space for a long time—weeks or months. Space stations are very large. Smaller spacecraft are used to carry people between Earth and the space station.

Other spacecraft are used to supply the station with food, water, equipment, and mail.

A space station orbits Earth hundreds of miles above Earth's surface. It also may be used as an observatory, factory, and warehouse.

In 1975, a U.S. Apollo spacecraft linked up with a Soviet Soyuz spacecraft. For the first time, crews from two different countries worked together in space. Since then, the many countries involved in space exploration have cooperated often.

The U.S. Unity, *right*, and the Russian Zarya, *left*, linked up in space to form part of the International Space Station in December 1998.

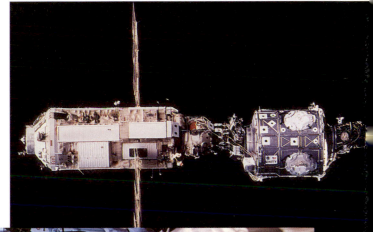

These cosmonauts on the space station Mir are securing equipment to be transferred to the space shuttle Atlantis.

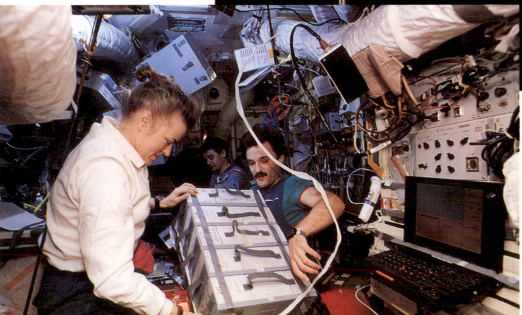

What Are Space Shuttles?

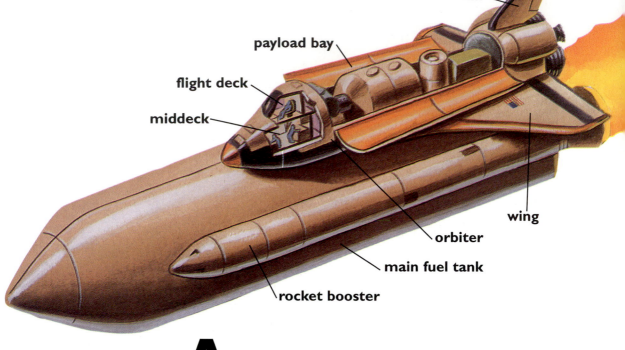

tail

payload bay

flight deck

middeck

wing

orbiter

main fuel tank

rocket booster

A space shuttle is a winged rocket plane. It can land on ordinary airfields, and so it can be used many times.

A space shuttle is used to launch satellites. It also recovers damaged satellites and returns them to Earth. It may be used to carry people or supplies to a space station, too.

When it is launched, a shuttle's nose is pointing toward the sky. It is powered by rocket booster motors and powerful engines. All five motors are started together. After a few minutes, the empty rocket boosters fall away and parachute into the sea. They are then recovered to use again.

Just before going into orbit, the shuttle's main fuel tank falls away. Smaller fuel tanks provide the rest of the energy needed. When the shuttle returns to Earth, it glides down without using any fuel.

Flight crews do most of their work on the flight deck. They prepare meals and sleep on the middeck. The shuttle's cargo is carried in the payload bay.

The word *shuttle* describes something that moves back and forth between two places, for example, shuttle buses. This is exactly what space shuttles do, too.

Do You Want to Work in Space?

The word *astronaut* comes from Greek words that mean "sailor among the stars." *Cosmonaut* means "sailor of the universe."

Today, astronauts and cosmonauts come from many countries of the world. But it is not easy to qualify to work in space. You must have a college degree in subjects related to space travel, such as math or science. There is no age limit, but to become an astronaut, you must pass the space flight **physical** (FIHZ uh kuhl) given by the National Aeronautics and Space Administration (NASA). A physical is a test or series of tests that determines a person's health.

There are two kinds of U.S. astronauts: pilots and mission specialists. Either one must be between 5 feet 4 inches and 6 feet 4 inches (163 and 193 centimeters) tall.

If you want to pilot a spacecraft, you need to spend at least 1,000 hours piloting a special type of jet aircraft.

Mission specialists must have spent at least three years doing the kind of work they will do on a mission. Some mission

This girl is riding the Multi-Axis at U.S. Space Camp in Huntsville, Alabama.

specialists operate and repair machinery and instruments in space. Others carry out experiments and tests to find out how things work in space. Others study the stars.

Russian astronauts are called cosmonauts. The first cosmonauts were military pilots and flight instructors. Most were in their early 20's.

Since Valentina Tereshkova's 1963 flight, crews of cosmonauts have included scientists and doctors. The first cosmonauts spent less than two years in training. Today, cosmonauts spend 8 to 10 years preparing for space flight. They train at the Y. A. Gagarin Center, also called "Star Town," near Moscow.

Training for Space

NASA's Space Shuttle Training Aircraft and a T-38 chase plane train over White Sands, New Mexico.

How does someone train to travel in space?

In the United States, both pilots and mission specialists spend one year of general training at the Johnson Space Center in Texas. Cosmonauts train at the Y. A. Gagarin Center, near Moscow, Russia. At the Johnson Space Center, the training has several parts. One part is classroom work. Students take special courses in topics related to space travel.

Another part is flight training in jet planes. This gives student pilots a chance to practice flying. Students who are training to become mission specialists do not pilot a jet during take-off and landing. But while the jet is in the air, they spend time at the controls.

Students also spend time on special jets that dive through the air. For about 30 seconds, the astronauts feel as if they

A special suit makes this astronaut feel like she's walking in space while underwater.

don't weigh anything at all. This prepares them for the way they will feel when they are in space—weightless.

Survival training is also part of the program. Students learn how to survive in the forest or in the water. They do this in case they have to make an emergency landing on Earth.

Early cosmonauts began with two months of very difficult activities that included high diving, skiing, wrestling, and parachuting. They also had difficult training in machines that made them experience extreme heat, gravity, and spinning motion.

This space crew is practicing water survival skills in the Black Sea. The skills would be needed if their spacecraft landed in the water rather than on land.

When the first astronauts began traveling in space, they ate foods like bite-sized cubes, freeze-dried powders, and thick liquid stuffed into tubes. Most astronauts agreed that it didn't taste very good. But these days, scientists know much more about what—and how—to feed astronauts. Here are a few examples of what packaged foods astronauts can eat in space today:

Foods to heat and eat:
beef steak
broccoli
eggs
green beans
macaroni and cheese
meatballs
rice and chicken
tomatoes
turkey

Snack foods:
candy
chocolate
 pudding
cookies
crackers
jelly
peanuts

As scientists have learned more about space, cosmonauts no longer need to be tested in such difficult ways. Now cosmonauts spend most of their time studying spacecraft and working in machines that are like imitation spacecraft.

During mission training, students study the cockpit of a spacecraft and are asked to perform certain tasks as if they were in space. A student who does well in all this training may be accepted as an astronaut!

Growing Food Without Soil

Space stations may grow food in unusual ways. Here's a simple activity you can do on Earth. Sprout your own seeds without soil.

What To Do:

1. Sprinkle a single layer of seeds into the bottom of the jar.

You Will Need:

an empty glass jar
cheesecloth
a rubber band
alfalfa seeds (from a garden store or health food store)
water

2. Cover the seeds with water. Stretch a double layer of cheesecloth over the jar's top and hold it on with the rubber band. Soak the seeds overnight.

3. Drain the water through the cheesecloth. Pound the jar to make the seeds fall back down or stick to the sides.

4. Let the jar sit for a few hours—not in direct sunlight.

5. Pour water in the jar again, through the cloth. Drain it out right away. Do this twice a day now, pounding your seeds down and still keeping the jar away from the sun.

Your seeds should begin to sprout in a day or two. When they are about 1 inch (2.5 cm) long, your sprouts are ready to eat. Toss them in a salad or on a sandwich.

Blast Off

Spaceflights are very exciting—from the preparation, launch, and spacewalks, all the way to the landing. This photo story shows astronauts on the first U.S. flight to help build the International Space Station (ISS).

The Unity module moves into the Space Shuttle Endeavour's payload bay. The crew's mission is to bring the module into space and connect it to another ISS module that is already in orbit.

The Endeavour undergoes final preparations atop the mobile launcher platform and crawler transporter. At the left are the pad's Rotating and Fixed Service Structures.

Technicians at the Kennedy Space Center's firing room receive and provide information to prepare for space launches and to monitor U.S. spacecraft throughout their missions.

The Space Shuttle Endeavour lifts off from Kennedy Space Center December 4, 1998, at 3:35:34 a.m.

While in orbit, the crew deployed Unity from the shuttle's payload bay and attached it to the Russian-built Zarya control module. The crew joined in space the first two parts of the International Space Station. The Unity is a connecting passageway to the living and working areas of the International Space Station.

The crew watched from Endeavour as the connected Zarya and Unity modules float away in the clouds after having been released from the shuttle cargo bay.

The Space Shuttle Endeavour touches down at Kennedy Space Center December 15, 1998, after an 11-day, 19-hour and 18-minute mission.

The triumphant crew gathers in front of the orbiter Endeavour after completing their successful mission. From left are mission specialists Jerry L. Ross and Nancy J. Currie, pilot Frederick "Rick" W. Sturckow, commander Robert D. Cabana, mission specialist James H. Newman, and Russian cosmonaut Sergei Konstantinovich Krikalev.

181

This glittering treasure chest of stars is in the heart of the Milky Way Galaxy, as viewed by the Hubble.

Hubble Space Telescope

Seeing Even Farther

Some objects are so far away and so faint in our sky that we can't see them clearly, even with the most powerful telescopes on Earth. But scientists have found two ways to view such distant objects: **space probes** and **space telescopes**.

A space probe is a spacecraft with no people on board. A probe may go far out into space, or it may land on a planet or moon. Some space probes bring samples back to Earth. Others make one-way journeys, sending back photos and information.

A space telescope is a telescope that stays in space. NASA launched the Hubble Space Telescope from a space shuttle in 1990. The Hubble orbits Earth about 380 miles (610 kilometers) above the surface. It is controlled by radio commands from NASA. The telescope can observe objects 50 times fainter than telescopes on Earth can. It also studies ultraviolet light that is blocked by Earth's atmosphere.

The Galileo space probe orbiting Jupiter